LANDLORDS' RIGHTS & DUTIES IN TEXAS

with forms

LANDLORDS' RIGHTS & DUTIES IN TEXAS

with forms

Second Edition

———

William R. Brown
Mark Warda
Attorneys at Law

SPHINX® PUBLISHING

A Division of Sourcebooks, Inc.®

Naperville, IL • Clearwater, FL

Second Edition, 2000

Published by: **Sphinx® Publishing, A Division of Sourcebooks, Inc.®**

<u>Naperville Office</u>
P.O. Box 4410
Naperville, Illinois 60567-4410
630-961-3900
Fax: 630-961-2168

<u>Clearwater Office</u>
P.O. Box 25
Clearwater, Florida 33757
727-587-0999
Fax: 727-586-5088

Interior and Cover Design: Sourcebooks, Inc.®
Interior and Cover Production: Amy S. Hall, Sourcebooks, Inc.®

This publication is designed to provide accurate and authoritative information in regard to the subject matter covered. It is sold with the understanding that the publisher is not engaged in rendering legal, accounting, or other professional service. If legal advice or other expert assistance is required, the services of a competent professional person should be sought.

From a Declaration of Principles Jointly Adopted by a Committee of the
American Bar Association and a Committee of Publishers and Associations

This product is not a substitute for legal advice.

Disclaimer required by Texas statutes

Library of Congress Cataloging-in-Publication Data
Brown, William R.
    Landlords' rights and duties in Texas : with forms / William R. Brown, Mark Warda.--
2nd ed.
        p.   cm.
    Includes index.
    ISBN 1-57248-110-2 (pbk)
        1. Landlord and tenant--Texas--Popular works. I. Title: Landlords' rights and duties in
Texas. II. Warda, Mark. III. Title.

KFT1317.Z9 B76 2000
346.76404'34--dc21
                                                                                    99-053002

Printed and bound in the United States of America.

HS Paperback — 10 9 8 7 6 5 4 3 2 1

CONTENTS

USING SELF-HELP LAW BOOKS

Before using a self-help law book, you should realize the advantages and disadvantages of doing your own legal work, and understand the challenges and diligence that this requires.

THE GROWING TREND

Rest assured that you won't be the first or only person handling their own legal matter. For example, in some states, more than seventy-five percent of the people in divorces and other cases represent themselves. Because of the cost of legal services, this is a major trend and many courts are struggling to make it easier for people to represent themselves. However, some courts are not happy with people who do not use attorneys, and refuse to help them in any way. For some, the attitude is, "Go to the law library and figure it out for yourself."

We write and publish self-help law books to give people an alternative to the often complicated and confusing legal books found in most law libraries. We have made the explanations of the law as simple and easy to understand as possible. Of course, unlike an attorney advising an individual client, we cannot cover every conceivable possibility.

COST/VALUE ANALYSIS

Whenever you shop for a product or service, you are faced with various levels of quality and price. In deciding what product or service to buy, you make a cost/value analysis on the basis of your willingness to pay and the quality you desire.

When buying a car, you decide whether you want transportation, comfort, status, or sex appeal. Accordingly, you decide among such choices as a Neon, a Lincoln, a Rolls Royce, or a Porsche. Before making a decision, you usually weigh the merits of each option against the cost.

When you get a headache, you can take a pain reliever (such as aspirin) or go visit a medical specialist for a neurological examination. Given this choice, most people, of course, take a pain reliever, since it costs only pennies; whereas a medical examination costs hundreds of dollars and takes a lot of time. This is usually a logical choice because rarely is anything more than a pain reliever needed for a headache. But in some cases, a headache may indicate a brain tumor and failing to see a specialist right away can result in complications. Should everyone with a headache go to a specialist? Of course not, but people treating their own illnesses must realize that they are betting on the basis of their cost/value analysis of the situation. They are choosing the most logical option.

The same cost/value analysis must be made in deciding to do one's own legal work. Many legal situations are very straight forward, requiring a simple form and no complicated analysis. Anyone with a little intelligence and a book of instructions can handle the matter without outside help.

But there is always the chance that complications are involved that only an attorney would notice. To simplify the law into a book like this, several legal cases often must be condensed into a single sentence or paragraph. Otherwise, the book would be several hundred pages long and too complicated for most people. However, this simplification necessarily leaves out many details and nuances that would apply to special or unusual situations. Also, there are many ways to interpret most legal questions. Your case may come before a judge who disagrees with the analysis of our authors.

Therefore, in deciding to use a self-help law book and to do your own legal work, you must realize that you are making a cost/value analysis. You are deciding that the money you will save outweighs the chance that your case will not turn out to your satisfaction. Most people handling their own simple legal matters never have a problem, but occasionally people find that it ended up costing them more to have an attorney straighten out the situation than it would have if they had hired an attorney in the beginning. Keep this in mind while handling your case and be sure to consult an attorney if you feel you might need further guidance.

LOCAL RULES
AND PROCEDURES

The next thing to remember is that a book which covers the law for the entire nation, or even for an entire state, cannot possibly include every procedural difference of every jurisdiction. Whenever possible, we provide the exact form needed; however, in some areas, each county, or even each judge, may require unique forms or procedures. In our state books, our forms usually cover the majority of counties in a state, or are examples of the type of form which will be required. In our national books, our forms are sometimes even more general in nature, but are designed to give a good idea of the type of form that will be needed in most locations. However, keep in mind that your state, county, or judge may have a requirement, or use a form, that is not included in this book.

You should not necessarily expect to be able to get all of the information and resources you need solely from within the pages of this book. This book will serve as your guide, giving you specific information whenever possible and helping you to find out what else you will need to know. This is just like if you decided to build your own backyard deck. You might purchase a book on how to build decks. However, such a book would not include the building codes and permit requirements of every city, town, county, and township in the nation; nor would it include the lumber, nails, saws, hammers, and other materials and tools you would need to actually build the deck. You would use the book as your guide, and then do some work and research involving such matters as whether you need a permit of some kind, what type and grade of wood are available in your area, whether to use hand tools or power tools, and how to learn to use those tools.

Before using the forms in a book like this, you should check with your court clerk to see if there are any local rules you need to know, or local forms which are required. Often, such forms will require the same information as the forms in the book, but are merely laid out differently or use slightly different language. Sometimes, they will require additional information.

CHANGES IN THE LAW

Besides being subject to local rules and practices, the law is subject to change at any time. The courts and the legislatures of all fifty states are constantly revising the laws. It is possible that, while you are reading this book, some aspect of the law is being changed.

In most cases, the change will be of minimal significance. A form will be redesigned, additional information will be required, or a waiting period will be extended. As a result, you might need to revise a form, file an extra form, or wait out a longer time period; but these types of changes will not usually affect the outcome of your case. On the other hand, sometimes a major part of the law is changed, the entire law in a particular area is rewritten, or a case that was the basis of a central legal point is overruled. In such instances, your entire ability to pursue your case may be impaired.

Again, you should weigh the value of your case against the cost of an attorney and make a decision of what you feel is in your best interest.

INTRODUCTION

Texas' landlord/tenant laws are like a double-edged sword. If a landlord does not know about them, or ignores them, he or she can lose thousands of dollars in lost rent, penalties, and attorney's fees. However, a landlord who knows the law can use the procedures to simplify life and to save money. Knowledge is power, and knowing the laws governing rentals will give you the power to protect your rights and to deal with problems effectively.

Laws are written to be precise, not to be easily readable. This book explains the law in simple language so that Texas landlords can know what is required of them and know their rights under the law. If you would like more detail about a law you can check the statutes in appendix A or research the court cases as explained in chapter 1.

Nearly every session the Texas legislature passes new laws regulating landlord/tenant relations and the courts of the state write more opinions defining the rights of landlords and tenants. To keep this book current and useful, this second edition was prepared for early 2000 release and includes the recent statutory and case law changes. This new edition was also completely reorganized to make the material easier to use and answers easier to find.

No book of this type can be expected to cover every situation that may arise. Laws change and different judges have different interpretations of what the laws mean. Only your lawyer, reviewing the unique characteristics of your situation, can give you an opinion of how the laws apply to your case. But this book can give you the legal framework to avoid costly mistakes.

When following the procedures in this book it should be kept in mind that different counties have different customs and some judges have their own way of doing things, so the requirements in your area may differ somewhat from those outlined in this book. Clerks and judge's assistants cannot give you legal advice, but often they can tell you what they require in order to proceed with your case. Before filing any forms, ask if your court provides its own forms or has any special requirements.

We at Sourcebooks hope that you find this book useful and we welcome your comments on this or any of our books.

Laws That Govern Rental Property

1

Texas Landlord/Tenant Law

Texas landlord/tenant law consists of both statutes passed by the legislature and legal opinions written by judges. The statutes usually address specific issues that have come up repeatedly in landlord/tenant relations. The judicial opinions interpret the statutes and decide what the law is in areas not specifically covered by statutes.

Unfortunately, sometimes the law is not clear. Since the statutes were written at different times by different legislators, they sometimes conflict. There are also local ordinances and agency regulations that may conflict with those laws, and judges do not always interpret them in the same way. You may encounter a situation where a judge or government official tells you to do something that you don't think is legally correct. Fortunately, this is a rare occasion, but if it happens to you, your two choices are to fight the issue in a higher court or to give in and do what is demanded. Most small landlords cannot afford a long court battle, so the only practical solution is to relent. Because of the cost in both time and money, and the uncertainty of the legal system, it is usually better to work out a settlement with a tenant than to let an issue go to a building inspector or before a judge. This will be explained in more detail later in the book.

WHICH TEXAS LAWS APPLY?

Various chapters of the Texas Property Code affect the landlord/tenant relationship. Depending upon the type of property you are renting, one or more of the following chapters may apply:

- ☞ Chapter 24 Forcible Entry and Detainer. This chapter controls eviction procedures.
- ☞ Chapter 91 This chapter generally applies to landlords and tenants.
- ☞ Chapter 92 This chapter controls residential rentals.
- ☞ Chapter 93 This chapter regulates any nonresidential, or commercial, rentals.

APPLICABILITY OF CHAPTER 92

The residential portion of the Chapter 92 of the Property Code applies to most residential tenancies, but does not apply to hotels, motels, or rooming houses; religious, educational, geriatric, or medical facilities; transient rentals; condominium owners; or proprietary leases in cooperatives. It also does not apply to contracts to purchase property.

APPLICABILITY OF CHAPTER 93

The laws concerning commercial tenancies are contained primarily in Chapter 93 of the Texas Property Code and in the common (or judge made) law. This portion of the Property Code covering commercial leases is relatively short and does not cover many specific situations. Accordingly, except for Chapter 92 of the Property Code, general law concerning all types of tenancies applies to commercial tenancies. The rules of residential tenancies are more strict and pro-tenant than rules for nonresidential tenancies. The landlord could incorporate residential tenancy procedures into a commercial lease and would be seen by a court to have been extra generous with the tenant. Just be sure the court doesn't become confused and think you had to follow the residential procedures for the non-residential tenancy.

CASH RENTAL PAYMENTS

Under § 92.011, a landlord can require a tenant to make payment by check, money order, or other negotiable instrument, as long as such requirement is contained in a written lease. Otherwise, the landlord must accept timely cash payments, give the tenant a receipt, and enter payment and date in a record book.

A tenant, governmental entity, or civic organization acting on behalf of the tenant can sue the landlord for injunction, court costs, attorney's fees, and the greater of one month's rent or $500.

OCCUPANCY LIMITS

According to § 92.010, a landlord may not allow more than three adults per bedroom to occupy a rental unit, unless:

- ☛ The landlord is required by a state or federal housing law to allow a higher occupancy; or
- ☛ The adult is seeking temporary sanctuary from family violence for a period of no longer than one month (in other words, a women's shelter is exempt)

If this occupancy limit is violated, a neighbor living in or owning a dwelling within 3,000 feet, a government entity, or a civic association acting for such a neighbor can sue the landlord for an injunction, court costs, attorney's fees, and a $500 penalty.

LOCAL LAWS

In some areas, local governments have passed various rules regulating landlords. Be sure to check with both your city and county governments for any local laws.

FEDERAL LAWS

Federal laws that apply to the rental of real estate include discrimination laws such as the Civil Rights Act, the Americans with Disabilities Act, and lead-based paint rules of the Environmental Protection Agency. These are explained in chapter 2 of this book. The United States Department of Housing and Urban Development (HUD) has a handbook that explains the rules applicable to public housing and other HUD programs.

DOING FURTHER RESEARCH

This book contains a summary of Texas Code statutes and court cases which affect landlord/tenant law in Texas. However, you may want to research your situation further by reading the entire statute section or court case. To do this, you will need the Code section number, or the *case citation* of the court case. Texas Code citations will indicate the title of the particular code (e.g., Property Code, Probate Code), and the section number, for example: "Property Code, § 83.49." Portions of the Texas landlord/tenant codes are included in appendix A in this book.

Court cases are noted in this book by the book symbol 📖. Case citations give you the name of the case, the volume and page of the reporter, and the court and year. For example, *Blackshear Residents Organization v. Housing Authority of the City of Austin*, 347 F.Supp. 1138 (W.D.Tex. 1972), means that the case titled *Blackshear Residents*

Organization v. Housing Authority of the City of Austin is found in volume 347 of the set of books titled *Federal Supplement* (abbreviated "F.Supp."), beginning on page 1138; and that it is a 1972 case from the Federal District Court for the Western District of Texas.

When reading the law contained in judges' opinions, be sure to note from which court the opinion originated. If it is not from a court which covers your geographical area, it might not be binding on your case. Supreme Court of Texas opinions apply to all courts in Texas, but Texas Court of Appeal opinions only apply to the geographical area they cover.

To learn more about doing legal research, you should refer to a book on the subject, such as *Legal Research Made Easy*, by Suzan Herskowitz, which is available through your local bookstore, or directly from Sphinx Publishing by calling 1-800-226-5291.

GOOD FAITH OBLIGATION

Every residential rental agreement, and every duty under the landlord/tenant law, requires "good faith" which is defined as "honesty in fact." Any sort of dishonesty or trickery could cause a loss of valuable rights. While this requirement is not in the nonresidential law (chapter 93), any lack of good faith in a nonresidential tenancy would likely have just as bad consequences for the perpetrator.

ASSUMED NAMES

Anyone doing business in Texas under a name other than his or her own personal name must register the name at the county Assumed Name Office. According to Business and Commercial Code §§ 36.10 and 36.11, a corporation, partnership, or limited liability company that uses an assumed name must register with the Secretary of State and the county Assumed Name Office. This applies to landlords who use "management company" names or apartment building names. The registration lasts for ten years and may be renewed. If a business is sold, the old registration may be assigned and the name re-registered.

CREATING THE LANDLORD/TENANT RELATIONSHIP 2

SCREENING PROSPECTIVE TENANTS

The first step in avoiding legal problems with tenants is to carefully choose who will be your tenant. As long as you do not discriminate based on such categories as race, sex, and age (see pages 14-19), you can be selective in to whom you rent your property. For example, a tenant who has had the same apartment and job for the last five years will probably be a better risk than one who has been evicted several times.

TENANT APPLICATION
You should get a written application from all prospective tenants. Besides allowing you to check their past record as a tenant, the information can be helpful in tracking them down if they disappear owing you rent or damages. (See form 1.) Be sure that the form you use does not ask illegal questions such as "nationality."

BACKGROUND INVESTIGATION
You should check with a prior landlord to see if he or she would rent to your prospective tenant again. Don't rely on a positive reference from their present landlord, who may lie just to get rid of them! And be sure the people you talk to are really landlords. Some tenants use friends to pose as their landlord and lie for them.

There are some companies which, for a fee, will investigate tenants including employment, previous landlords, court cases, and the company's own files of "bad tenants." Some landlords require a non-refundable application fee to cover such an investigation. Tenant Check is one company which screens tenants. Call them toll free at 1-888-244-7761, or visit one of their websites:

Tenant Check: http://www.infotel.net/tenantcheck

Tenant Check links: http://www.infotel.net/tenantcheck/tclinks.htm

Tenant Check home page: http://posidon.net/tc/form.html

CBI/Equifax offers a Tenant Apartment Protection Service (call them toll free at 1-800-388-0456.

CREDIT
REPORTS

You may also wish to obtain a credit report on a prospective tenant. By law, the tenant must be informed of the potential of a credit check and give permission for a credit report. Once you have such permission, you can contact a local credit bureau such as Equifax, TRW, or Trans Union; or contact a company that runs credit checks, such as American Tenant Screen (1-800-888-1287) and Rent Grow (1-800-736-8476, ext. 400). CBI/Equifax offers a Tenant Apartment Protection Service (1-800-388-0456). Otherwise, check your phone book under Credit Reporting Agencies.

DISCRIMINATION

Since Congress passed the Civil Rights Act of 1968, it has been a federal crime for a landlord to discriminate in the rental or sale of property on the basis of race, religion, sex, or national origin. In addition, Texas passed its own anti-discrimination statute which makes such acts a state crime and adds the additional category of handicapped persons. In 1988, the United States Congress passed an amendment to the Civil Rights Act that bans discrimination against both the handicapped and families with children. Except for apartment complexes which fall into the special exceptions, all rentals must now allow children in all units.

CIVIL RIGHTS ACT OF 1968	Under the Civil Rights Act of 1968 (42 USC 3601-17) any policy which has a discriminatory effect is illegal.

PENALTY. A victim of discrimination under this section can file a civil suit, a HUD complaint, or request the U.S. Attorney General to prosecute. Damages can include actual losses and punitive damages of up to $1,000. Failure to attend a hearing or to produce records can subject you to up to a year in prison or $1,000 fine.

LIMITATION. The complaint must be brought within 180 days.

EXEMPTIONS. This law does not apply to single-family homes if the owner owns three or less; if there is no more than one sale within twenty-four months; if the person does not own any interest in more than three at one time; and if no real estate agent or discriminatory advertisement is used. It also does not apply to a property that the owner lives in if it has four or less units.

COERCION OR INTIMIDATION. Where coercion or intimidation is used to effectuate discrimination, there is no limit to when the action can be brought or the amount of damages. For example, one real estate agent was fired for renting to African-Americans. *Wilkey v. Pyramid Construction Co.*, 619 F.Supp. 1453 (D. Conn. 1983).

CIVIL RIGHTS ACT § 1982

The Civil Rights Act §1982 (42 USC 1982) is similar to the above statute but where the above applies to any policy which has a discriminatory effect, this law applies only where it can be proved that the person had an intent to discriminate.

PENALTY. Actual damages plus unlimited punitive damages.

In 1992, a jury in Washington, D.C., awarded civil rights groups $850,000 damages against a developer who only used Caucasian models in rental advertising. *The Washington Post* now requires that the models in ads it accepts must be twenty-five percent African-America to reflect the percentage of African-American's in the Washington area.

LIMITATIONS AND EXEMPTIONS. None.

CIVIL RIGHTS
ACT 1988
AMENDMENT

The 1988 Amendment to the Civil Rights Act (42 USC 3601) bans discrimination against the handicapped and families with children. Unless a property falls into one of the exemptions, it is illegal under this law to refuse to rent to persons because of age or to refuse to rent to children. While landlords may be justified in feeling that children cause damage to their property which they wish to avoid, Congress has ruled that the right of families to find housing is more important than the rights of landlords in the condition of their property. The exemptions are for two types of housing: 1) Where the units are rented solely by persons sixty-two or older; 2) Where eighty percent of the units are rented to persons fifty-five or older. In late 1995, the law was amended so that the property does not need to have special facilities for such persons' needs.

Regarding the disabled, the law allows them to remodel the unit to suit their needs as long as they return it to the original condition upon leaving. It also requires new buildings of four units or more to have electrical facilities and common areas accessible to the disabled.

PENALTY. $10,000 for first offense, $25,000 for second violation within five years and up to $50,000 for three or more violations within seven years. Unlimited punitive damages in private actions.

LIMITATION. Complaint can be brought within two years for private actions.

EXEMPTIONS. This law does not apply to single-family homes if the owner owns three or less, if there is no more than one sale within twenty-four months, if the person does not own any interest in more than three at one time, and if no real estate agent or discriminatory advertisement is used. (A condominium unit is not a single-family home so is not exempt.) It also does not apply to a property the owner lives in if it has four or less units. Additionally, there are exemptions for dwellings in state and federal programs for the elderly, for complexes that are solely used by persons sixty-two or older, and for complexes used solely by persons fifty-five or over if there are substantial facilities designed for the elderly, for religious housing and for private clubs.

AMERICANS WITH
DISABILITIES ACT

The Americans with Disabilities Act (ADA) requires that "reasonable accommodations" be made to provide the disabled with access to commercial premises and forbids discrimination against them. This means that the disabled must be able to get to, enter, and use the facilities in commercial premises. It requires that if access is "readily achievable" without "undue burden" or "undue hardship," changes must be made to the property to make it accessible. Fortunately, the ADA does not apply to residential rental property.

Under the ADA, if any commercial premises are remodeled, then the remodeling must include modifications that make the premises accessible. All new construction must also be made accessible.

The law does not clearly define important terms like *reasonable accommodations, readily achievable, undue burden,* or *undue hardship,* and does not even explain exactly who will qualify as handicapped or disabled. Some claim that up to forty percent of America's labor force may qualify as handicapped. The law includes people with emotional illnesses, AIDS, dyslexia, and past alcohol or drug addictions; as well as hearing, sight, and mobility impairments. Of course, this law will provide lots of work for lawyers who will sue landlords and businesses.

What is reasonable will usually depend upon the size of the business. Small businesses will not have to make major alterations to their premises if the expense would be an undue hardship. Even large businesses wouldn't need shelving low enough for people in wheelchairs to reach, as long as there was an employee to assist the person.

However, there are tax credits for businesses of less than thirty employees and less than one million dollars in sales which make modifications to comply with the ADA. For more information on these credits, obtain IRS forms 8826 and 3800 and their instructions.

Some of the changes that must be made to property to make it more accessible to the disabled are:

☞ Installing ramps
☞ Widening doorways

☛ Making curb cuts in sidewalks

☛ Repositioning shelves

☛ Repositioning telephones

☛ Removing high pile, low density carpeting

☛ Installing a full-length bathroom mirror

Both the landlord and the tenant can be liable if the changes are not made to the premises. Most likely, the landlord would be liable for common areas and the tenant for the area under her control. However, since previous leases did not address this new statute either party could conceivably be held liable.

PENALTY. Injunctions and fines of $50,000 for the first offense or $100,000 for subsequent offenses.

EXEMPTIONS. Private clubs and religious organizations are exempt from this law.

TEXAS DISCRIMINATION LAW

The Texas Fair Housing Act, Chapter 301 of the Texas Property Code, prohibits rental discrimination based on race, religion, sex, national origin, handicap, or *familial status* (meaning whether the tenant has children). The provisions are similar to federal laws.

Assistance Animals. A landlord must rent to a disabled person with an assistance animal/support dog even if she has a general no pets rule. She cannot charge additional rent for the assistance animal, but can charge an additional pet deposit. (Human Resources Code, § 121.003.)

Local Laws. Landlords should also check their city and county ordinances before adopting a discriminatory policy.

The following cases can give some guidance as to what types of actions are outlawed or permitted.

📖 It is illegal to segregate the people in an apartment complex. *Blackshear Residents Organization v. Housing Authority of the City of Austin*, 347 F.Supp. 1138 (W.D.Tex. 1972).

📖 It is considered sex discrimination to not include child support and alimony in an applicant's income. *U.S. v. Reese*, 457 F.Supp. 43 (D. Mont. 1978).

📖 It is not illegal to require a single parent and a child of the opposite sex to rent a two-bedroom rather than a one-bedroom apartment. *Braunstein v. Dwelling Managers, Inc.*, 476 F.Supp. 1323 (S.D.N.Y. 1979).

📖 It was found not to be illegal to limit the number of children allowed. *Fred v. Koknokos*, 347 F.Supp. 942 (E.D.N.Y. 1972). (But there may be a different interpretation under the 1988 amendment. Also, be sure to check local ordinances.)

📖 A company that used only caucasian models in its housing ads was ordered to pay $30,000 in damages. (The judge overruled the jury's recommended $262,000!) *Ragin v. Macklowe*, No. 88 Civ. 5665 (RWS), S.D.N.Y., Aug. 25, 1992.

AGREEMENTS TO LEASE

What are your rights if a tenant agrees to rent your unit but then reneges? The landlord/tenant relationship is created by an agreement to lease. An agreement to enter into a lease may be a valid and binding contract even if a lease has not yet been signed. We recommend you have a written agreement.

As a practical matter, it will probably not be worth the time and expense to sue someone for breaching an oral agreement to lease. Whether or not a landlord could keep a deposit after a prospective tenant changed her mind would depend upon the facts of the case an the understanding between parties. Writing "non-refundable" on the deposit receipt would work in the landlord's favor.

LEASES AND RENTAL AGREEMENTS

There are different opinions as to whether a landlord should use a lease with a set term, such as one year, or a month-to-month lease. Some argue that they would rather have a month-to-month lease so they can get rid of a tenant with thirty days notice. The disadvantage is that the tenant can also leave with thirty days notice, which means the unit may be vacant during the slow season.

RENTAL
AGREEMENTS

In all cases, there should be a written agreement between the parties. If the landlord does not want to tie up the property for a long period of time, he or she can use a Month-to-Month Lease (form 6), which states that the tenancy is month-to-month, but which also includes rules and regulations to protect the landlord.

LEASES

A lease is a rental agreement which is for a set term. It can be as short as a few weeks or for several years.

REQUIRED
CLAUSES

The minimum elements which a lease must contain to be valid are:

- ☛ The name of the lessor (landlord) or agent
- ☛ The name of the lessee (tenant)
- ☛ A description of the premises
- ☛ The rental rate
- ☛ The starting and ending date (term of lease)
- ☛ A *granting clause* (this is a statement that clearly indicates a lease is created, such as a sentence beginning: "Lessor hereby leases to Lessee the premises located at...")

(Actually, there have been cases where a lease has been held to be valid where one or more of these terms has been omitted if there was an objective means to determine the missing term, but such exceptions are beyond the scope of this book.)

OWNERSHIP AND
MANAGEMENT
DISCLOSURE

Some landlords have attempted to avoid being sued by tenants by hiding behind management companies. If the tenant doesn't know the landlord, he or she can't sue the landlord. The legislature has attempted to correct this problem by passing a residential landlord disclosure law. Residential landlords are required to disclose to a tenant the name and address of the record owner of the dwelling, according to the deed records, and, if applicable, the name and address of any off-site management company managing the unit. This disclosure can be made by the following methods:

1. Including the information in the lease or written rules given to the tenant

2. Giving the information in writing to the tenant within seven days of the tenant's request

3. Posting the information in the dwelling, in the management office, or on the door to the management office within seven days of the tenant's request

If the landlord fails to give the required information, or fails to correct any incorrect information, the tenant can terminate the lease and recover any actual damages incurred in discovering the information, plus one month's rent, a $100 penalty, attorney's fees, and court costs. If the tenant owes rent on the day he or she makes a request for information, the landlord will not be liable; however, if the landlord willfully fails to give the information or knowingly gives incorrect information, the violation is considered in bad faith, and rent delinquency is not a defense (§§92.204 and 92.206). The parties may not waive these rights and duties (§ 92.006).

LEAD PAINT DISCLOSURE

In 1996, the Environmental Protection Agency and the Department of Housing and Urban Development issued regulations requiring notices to be given to tenants of rental housing built before 1978 that there may be lead-based paint present and that it could pose a health hazard to children. This applies to all housing except housing for the elderly or zero-bedroom units (efficiencies, studio apartments, etc.) It also requires that a pamphlet about lead-based paint, titled *Protect Your Family From Lead in Your Home* be given to prospective tenants. The recommended disclosure form is included in this book as form 29.

The rule is contained in the *Federal Register*, Vol. 61, No. 45, March 6, 1996, pages 9064-9088. More information, and copies of the pamphlet, can be obtained from the National Lead Information Clearinghouse at 1-800-424-5323. The information can also be obtained at the following website: http://www.nsc.org/nsc/ehc/ehc.html.

SUGGESTED CLAUSES

The following types of clauses are not required by any law, but are suggested by the authors to avoid potential problems during the tenancy.

☛ Security or damage deposit

☛ Last month's rent

☛ Use clause (limiting use of the property)

☛ Maintenance clause (spelling out who is responsible for which area of maintenance)

☛ Limitation on landlord's liability

☛ Limitation on assignment of the lease by tenant

☛ Clause granting attorney's fees for enforcement of the lease

☛ Clause putting duty on tenant for own insurance

☛ Late fee and fee for bounced checks

☛ Limitation on number of persons living in the unit

☛ In a condominium or apartment, a clause stating that tenant must comply with all rules and regulations of the condominium

☛ Requirement that if locks are changed landlord is given a key (forbidding tenants to change locks may subject the landlord to liability for a break-in)

☛ Limitation on pets (see the Pet Agreement, form 3 in appendix C)

☛ Limitation on where cars may be parked (not on the lawn, etc.)

☛ Limitation on storage of boats, etc. on the property

☛ In a single family home or duplex a landlord should put most of the duties for repair on the tenant

☞ In commercial leases, there should be clauses regarding the fixtures, insurance, signs, renewal, eminent domain and other factors related to the business use of the premises

☞ An abandoned property clause (see the section on "Property Abandoned by Tenant" in chapter 8)

For an explanation and analysis of each of the different clauses used in residential and commercial leases and suggestions on how to negotiate, see *How to Negotiate Real Estate Leases*, by Mark Warda, available through your local bookstore, or directly from Sphinx Publishing by calling 1-800-226-5291.

ORAL LEASES
A lease of property for less than one year does not have to be in writing to be valid. Oral leases have been held up in court. The problem will be in proving the terms of your agreement, since it will often be the tenant's word against the landlord's. In these situations, it will just depend upon who sounds more believable to the judge.

IMPLIED LEASES
Even without an express oral or written contract, and even without an agreement to pay rent, an *implied tenancy* can be created if the tenant takes possession of the property with the landlord's consent. Therefore, landlords should make sure a lease is signed, and the first month's rent and any security deposit is paid, before giving a tenant the keys.

PERPETUAL LEASES
Leases which are renewable indefinitely are not favored by courts. Where doubt exists as to the terms, they may be limited to one renewal term.

PROBLEM CLAUSES

UNCONSCIONABLE
If a judge feels that a rental agreement is grossly unfair, he or she may rule that it is *unconscionable*, and therefore unenforceable. In such a case, the judge may ignore the entire lease or may enforce only parts of it. Therefore, making your lease too strong may defeat your purpose. There is not much guidance as to what may or may not be unconscionable, so the judge may use his discretion.

📖 A cost of living adjustment in the rent was found not to be unconscionable. *Bennett v. Behring Corp.*, 466 F.Supp. 689 (1979).

HIDDEN
CLAUSES

If a lease contains a clause which might be considered controversial, it should not be buried in the lease. It should be pointed out to, and initialed by, the tenant.

WAIVERS IN
COMMERCIAL
LEASES

In a commercial lease, a tenant may waive rights which may not be waived in a residential lease. A commercial lease spells out nearly all of the rights and obligations of the parties. The statutes concerning landlord/tenant law are very limited in scope so it is important to spell everything out carefully in the lease.

LIMITING
SIMILAR
BUSINESSES

Some tenants request a provision which limits the landlord's right to lease to similar types of businesses. These provisions are strictly construed by the courts. For example, where a lease provides that a lessee would be the only "appliance store" in a shopping center, it may be legal for the landlord to lease to a department store which also sells ranges, refrigerators, freezers, and other appliances.

OPTIONS

OPTIONS TO
RENEW

Residential and nonresidential leases may contain clauses granting the tenant an option to extend the lease for another term or several terms. Often these options provide for an increase in rent during the renewal periods. An option to renew a lease is valid and enforceable, even if not all of the terms are outlined. Some terms may be left open for future negotiation or arbitration, but where no terms are stated, the court can assume that the terms will be the same terms as in the original lease (so be sure to draft your options carefully!). As stated earlier, leases which can be renewed indefinitely are not favored by the courts, and where doubt exists as to the terms, they may be limited to one renewal term.

OPTIONS TO
PURCHASE

If a lease contains an option to purchase, it will usually be enforceable exactly according to its terms.

FORMS

The landlord should be careful to choose a good lease form. Some forms on the market do not comply with Texas law and can be dangerous to use. Forms 4, 5, and 6 in this book are leases developed and used by the authors. These forms are free of legalese and intended to be easily understandable by both parties. You may also need to use form 29 as explained elsewhere in the text.

SIGNATURES

If you do not have the proper signatures on the lease you could have problems enforcing it, or evicting the tenants.

LANDLORD If the property is owned by more than one person, it is best to have all owners sign the lease. If the owner is a corporation, the lease should be signed by an authorized officer or agent of the corporation. For property owned by a Limited Liability Company, the lease should be signed by an authorized member or agent of the LLC. If the property is owned by a partnership, any partner or an authorized agent may sign.

TENANT In most cases, it is best to have all adult occupants sign the lease so that more people will be liable for the rent. But in inexpensive rentals, where evictions are frequent, having just one person sign will save a few dollars in fees for service of process.

INITIALS Some landlords have places on the lease for the tenant to place their initials. This is usually done next to clauses which are unusual or very strongly pro-landlord or if terms are changed. This can defeat a tenant's argument that he or she didn't see the provision.

WITNESSES No witnesses are required for a lease of one year or less. A lease of over one year is not valid without two witnesses to the Landlord's signature. If a party accepts the benefits of a lease, even if it is not properly witnessed, that party may be "estopped" from contesting the lease's validity. A landlord was estopped in *Bodden v. Carbonell*, 354 So.2d 927 (Fla. 2 DCA 1978). A tenant was estopped in *Arvanetes v. Gilbert*, 143 So.2d 825 (Fla. 3 DCA 1962).

NOTARY

A lease does not need to be notarized to be valid. A landlord should not allow his signature on a lease to be notarized because the lease could then be recorded in the public records which would be a cloud on his title and could cause a problem when the property is sold.

BACKING OUT OF A LEASE

RESCISSION

Contrary to the beliefs of some tenants, there is no law allowing a rescission period for a lease. Once a lease has been signed by both parties, it is legally binding on them.

FRAUD

If one party fraudulently misrepresents a material fact concerning the lease, the lease may be unenforceable.

IMPOSSIBILITY

If the lease states that the premises are rented for a certain purpose and it is impossible to use the premises for that purpose, the lease may not be enforceable. For example, if property was rented for a storage business and the zoning laws made it illegal to operate the business on the premises, the landlord probably could not sue the tenant for failing to pay the rent. But if the tenant could not operate his business because of difficulty in getting insurance, this would not make it impossible to use the property and the tenant would still have to pay the rent.

ILLEGALITY

If a lease is entered into for an illegal purpose, then it is void and unenforceable by either party.

TYPES OF TENANCY

Texas law recognizes four basic types of tenancies: tenancy for a fixed term; periodic tenancy; tenancy at will; and tenancy at sufferance.

TENANCY FOR A
FIXED TERM

A *tenancy for a fixed term* is just what it says. It lasts from one date to another. It ends on that date unless the parties agree to renew it. It could terminate earlier based on some agreed upon condition, such as a sale of the premises.

PERIODIC
TENANCY

A *periodic tenancy* is usually of two types, a month to month or year to year. The month to month is more common. If the parties merely agree on occupancy of the premises with a monthly rent and don't set a definite end date, a month to month tenancy is created. A year to year tenancy would be created if the parties agreed on an annual rent with no set term.

A periodic tenancy can be created by a holding over with the landlord's consent. If a tenant holds over after the end of a one year lease, and the landlord accepts rent in accordance with the preexisting lease terms, the tenancy become a year to year tenancy, and the tenant can stay for another year at the same rent. However, if the landlord or tenant notified the other that any holdover is only for month to month, that's what it is. A landlord should include a provision in his lease that any holdover consented to by the landlord creates only a month to month tenancy. A month to month tenancy can be terminated by giving one month's notice. However, if the rent paying period is less than a month, the tenancy can be terminated after a notice equal to the number of days in the rent paying period. The parties can agree in the lease on a different notice period or even that no notice is required (§ 91.001).

TENANCY AT
WILL

A *tenancy at will* is created whenever the term is uncertain, such as when the lease permits the tenant to occupy the premises as long as she pays rent. A tenancy at will can be terminated by either party at any time.

TENANCY AT
SUFFERANCE

A *tenancy at sufferance* is created when a tenant under a term lease holds over after the term has expired. It can be terminated at any time unless the landlord has accepted rent creating a periodic tenancy as described above.

PETS

Because of the problems caused by pets, landlords usually forbid them unless written permission is granted and usually require additional security deposits for pets. Although it is illegal to discriminate against children, it is still legal to discriminate against pets. Though it is probably just a matter of time before a pets rights law is passed!

A Pet Agreement (form 3) is included in this book. However, there is one danger in keeping the right to control pets. If the landlord has the power to terminate a tenancy because a pet is a nuisance, the landlord may be liable if he doesn't evict the tenant and the pet injures someone.

NOTICE AT PRIMARY RESIDENCE

If a tenant gives the landlord notice, at the time of signing a lease or renewal, that it is not his primary residence and requests notice at his primary residence, the landlord must send him notices under the lease (§ 92.012).

APPLICATION DEPOSIT

If a tenant gives a landlord a deposit in connection with a rental application that is refundable if the application is rejected, the landlord is required to return the deposit if the application is rejected. An application is considered to be rejected if there is no acceptance by the seventh day after application or payment of an application deposit. A landlord who fails to return the deposit can be sued for $100, plus three times the amount of the application deposit, attorney's fees, and court costs (§ 92.351 et seq.).

HANDLING SECURITY DEPOSITS 3

This chapter on security deposits only applies to residential tenancies. Texas does not have statutes governing nonresidential security deposits. The laws concerning residential security deposits are found in the Texas Property Code, Section 92.101 et. seq.

AMOUNT

Unlike some states, Texas does not have a law limiting the amount of security deposit a landlord may require. The decision about how much of a deposit to charge must be made based on the practical consideration of what is the most you can get without scaring away desirable tenants.

BANK ACCOUNT, INTEREST, AND NOTICES

Again, unlike some states, Texas does not have any laws requiring where security deposits must be kept, mandating the payment of interest on security deposits, or requiring that any specific notices be given to tenants about where their deposits are being kept.

Keeping or Refunding the Deposit

A landlord must refund a security deposit within thirty days after the tenant moves out of the premises (§ 92.103). Any damages and charges under the lease may be deducted from the deposit, except for damages from normal wear and tear. If any of the security deposit is kept, the landlord must give the tenant a written description and itemized list of all deductions and refund any balance of the deposit. The description and itemized list is not required if the tenant owes rent when he or she moves out and the amount owed is not disputed (§ 92.104).

Notices by Tenant

The landlord need not provide the refund or description of damages and charges until the tenant gives the landlord written notice of his change of address (§ 92.107).

A written lease can require that the tenant give advance notice of surrender as a condition for receiving a refund of the security deposit, but such requirement must be either underlined or printed in conspicuous bold print (§ 92.103).

If Tenant Fails to Move In

If a tenant pays a security deposit or rent prepayment but does not move in, the landlord may not keep the money if the landlord or the tenant gets a replacement tenant (satisfactory to the landlord) who moves in by the date the original lease begins. The landlord can keep either an agreed upon cancellation fee or the landlord's actual expenses incurred in securing a replacement, including a reasonable amount of time in finding a replacement tenant.

Penalties

If a landlord fails to refund the security deposit or give the description of damages and charges within thirty days after the tenant moves out, the landlord is presumed to have acted in bad faith. If the tenant sues and the court finds the landlord retained the security deposit in bad faith, the landlord is liable for $100 plus three times the security deposit withheld and attorney's fees. If the landlord fails to provide the description of damages and charges in bad faith, the landlord cannot withhold any security deposit, cannot sue the tenant for damages, and will be liable for the tenant's attorney's fees (§ 92.109).

The parties cannot waive these rights and duties (§ 92.006).

If a tenant fails to pay the last month's rent, claiming that the security deposit is security for unpaid rent, he or she can be sued by the landlord for three times the unpaid rent plus attorney's fees (§ 92.108).

SALE OF THE PROPERTY

If the rental property is sold or otherwise transferred, except for in a foreclosure, the new owner is liable to the tenant for the security deposit. The old owner is also liable until the new owner accepts responsibility for the deposit in writing to the tenant (§ 92.105).

Responsibility for Maintenance 4

Nonresidential Rentals

Texas statutes do not specify who is responsible for maintenance in nonresidential rentals. All of the responsibilities should be spelled out in the lease.

Residential Tenancies

A landlord has a duty to repair a condition of the property that materially affects the physical health or safety of an ordinary tenant if the tenant gives the landlord notice of the condition and the tenant is not delinquent in paying rent. If the lease is written and requires written notice, the tenant's notice must be written. If the condition was caused by a tenant or guest of the tenant, the landlord does not have to repair it unless the condition was caused by normal wear and tear (§ 92.052).

The landlord is required to make a diligent effort to repair or remedy the condition within a reasonable time after receipt of notice to repair or remedy. There is a rebuttal presumption that seven days is a reasonable time. If the landlord has still not made the repairs, the tenant is required to give a subsequent written notice to repair. (The tenant can skip this second notice if he gives the first notice in writing by certified mail, return receipt requested, registered mail.) If after a reasonable time, the landlord has still not made the repairs, the tenant can exercise his remedies. He can (1) terminate the lease; (2) sue the landlord; or (3) make certain repairs himself and deduct the cost from the rent up to the greater of one month's rent or $500.

If the tenant sues, he can recover one month's rent plus $500, reduction in rent, actual damages, and attorney's fees, plus an order from the judge that the repairs be made. If the tenant terminates the lease and moves, he is entitled to a refund of rent from the date of termination or move out and a refund of his security deposit (§ 92.056).

If the tenant uses the repair and deduct remedy, either of the written notices given to the landlord must state that he intends to make the repairs himself. This repair option can be used for repair of (1) backup or overflow of raw sewage inside; (2) flooding from broken pipes or natural drainage inside; (3) no water service if the landlord has expressly or impliedly agreed to provide water; (4) inadequate heating or cooling and the local building officials have notified the landlord in writing that the lack of heat or cooling materially affects the health or safety of an ordinary tenant; or (5) the local housing and building officials have notified the landlord in writing that the condition materially affects the health or safety of an ordinary tenant. Repair of sewage backup can begin immediately after notice of intent to repair, repair of potable water and heating or cooling problems three days after notice, and any other health or safety problem within seven days after notice of intent to repair.

DUTY TO REPAIR   The parties can't waive the landlord's duty to repair, except that the parties can agree for the tenant to make repairs at the landlord's expense. Also, if the landlord owns only one rental property and that property is free of safety and health defects at the beginning of the lease term, and the landlord has not had reason to believe there are any problems with the property, the parties can agree in writing that the tenant will make and pay for repairs, as long as the language is clear and specific, underlined or in bold print, and the agreement was made knowingly and voluntarily and for consideration.

Also, all parties can agree that the tenant will pay for repairs of the following unless caused by the landlord's negligence:

- ☞ Waste water stoppages caused by foreign or improper objects in lines exclusively serving the tenant's dwelling

- ☞ Damages to doors, windows, or screens

- ☞ Damage from doors or windows left open

Such an agreement must be in writing, in bold or underlined print, clear and specific, made knowingly and voluntarily, and for *consideration*. (Consideration is a legal term meaning that there is an exchange of something of value. If the repair agreement is part of the lease, the consideration would be the tenant's agreement to lease for a certain price. If such an agreement is signed after the lease is signed, it would not have adequate consideration, and would, therefore, not be enforceable.) However, repair is the landlord's responsibility if a plumbing backup is caused by deterioration of the plumbing, roots, or malfunctioning equipment (§ 92.006).

LANDLORD'S
AFFIDAVIT FOR
DELAY

The landlord can prevent the tenant from making repairs under 92.0561 by delivering an affidavit to the tenant, where the landlord makes a sworn statement concerning the reason for delay and states facts showing the landlord has made and is making diligent efforts to repair the problem, including dates, names, addresses, and telephone numbers of repairmen, etc., contacted by the landlord (§ 92.0562).

After receiving such an affidavit, the tenant may not do repairs:

- ☞ for fifteen days if the delay is caused because a needed part is unavailable, or

- ☞ for thirty days if the delay is caused by a general labor or material shortage due to a natural disaster, such as tornado, hurricane, flood, extended freeze, or widespread windstorm.

If the cause of the delay continues, the landlord may deliver subsequent affidavits up to six months. The landlord must continue to use diligent efforts to complete the repairs. If the landlord violates this section, the tenant can sue for actual damages, attorney's fees, court costs, and a civil penalty equal to one month's rent plus $1,000.

The statute contains complicated rules for a new landlord who acquires the property after the tenant gives notice of repairs. If you are in this situation, review § 92.056(g) or consult an attorney.

CASUALTY LOSS
If a condition requiring repairs results from a casualty loss (such as fire, smoke, hail, etc.) that is covered by insurance, the repair period does not begin until the landlord receives the insurance proceeds (§ 92.054).

If the premises are totally unusable for residential purposes, and the loss is not caused by the fault of the tenant, his family, or guest; either party can terminate the lease by written notice to the other any time before repairs are completed. If the lease is terminated in this way, the tenant is entitled to a prorated refund of rent from the date of moving out, and a refund of his or her security deposit.

If the premises are partially unusable and the loss is not caused by the tenant's fault, the tenant is entitled to a reduced rent but must file suit to get a court determination of how much. The parties may agree otherwise in a written lease.

SECURITY DEVICES
Landlords of residential rental homes, duplexes, triplexes, apartments, condominiums, townhomes, cooperatives, certain mobile homes, and rooming houses and dormitories must provide, at their expense, certain security devices. Hotels, motels, and college dorms are exempt from these requirements. Each dwelling must have:

☞ A window latch on each exterior window

☞ A doorknob lock or keyed deadbolt on each exterior door

☞ A sliding door pinlock and either a sliding door handle latch or sliding door security bar on each exterior sliding door

☞ A keyless bolting device and door viewer on each exterior door

☛ French doors must have one door which meets the above requirements and the other door must have either (a) a keyed deadbolt of keyless bolting device capable of insertion into the doorjamb above the door and a keyless bolting device insertable into the floor or threshold, each with a bolt having a throw of one inch or more, or (b) one inside bolt operated from the edge of the door insertable into doorjamb above the door and one inside bolt operated from the edge of the door insertable in the floor or threshold, such having a throw of at least 3/4 inch.

A keyless bolting device is not required on exterior doors in multi-unit complexes for physically or mentally disabled tenants or tenants over fifty-five, if the lease permits or requires the landlord to check on the tenants periodically. Also, a keyless bolting device is not required if a tenant or occupant is over fifty-five years old or has a physical or mental disability, and the tenant requests, in a writing separate from the lease, that the keyless bolt be deactivated or not installed, and the tenant certifies that the tenant or occupant is over fifty-five or has a physical or mental disability.

If at least one normal entry door has a keyed deadbolt and a keyless bolting device, the other exterior doors only need a keyless bolting device.

The terms *keyless bolting device, keyed deadbolt, door viewer, doorknob lock, exterior door, sliding door handle latch, sliding door pin lock, sliding door security bar,* and *window latch* are all specifically defined in the statute (§ 92.151).

The statute has certain height, strike plate and throw requirements for keyed deadbolts and keyless bolting devices:

Height.

☛ At lease thirty-six inches, but not higher than fifty-four inches, if installed before 9-1-93

☛ At lease thirty-six inches, but not higher than forty-eight inches, if installed after 9-1-93

Strike Plate. Either a strike plate or a metal doorjamb.

Thrower. If installed after 9-1-93, a throw of at least one inch.

A sliding door pin lock or sliding door security bar must be installed no higher than (1) fifty-four inches if installed before 9-1-93; or (2) forty-eight inches if installed on or after 9-1-93.

The parties cannot waive these rights and duties (§ 92.006).

REKEYING AND
REPAIRING
SECURITY DEVICES
A landlord must rekey (at the landlord's expense) an exterior door lock within seven days after a tenant moves into a unit. If the tenant requests rekeying at any time, the landlord must do so at the tenant's expense (§ 92.156). The landlord is not required to rekey if the tenant has not fully paid rent on the day a request is made (§ 92.158). However, a landlord might be subjecting himself to a big lawsuit if he refuses to rekey because of unpaid rent and someone with an old key gets in and injures the tenant. The landlord might win, but is it worth the headache and expense?

A landlord must repair or replace inoperable security device upon request. The notice can be oral unless the written lease requires written notice (§ 92.159).

The landlord must rekey or repair within a reasonable time after receiving the request. Normally, that is no later than seven days after the request.

A landlord may require the tenant to pay for repair or replacement (unless caused by normal wear and tear) only if a written lease with an underlined provision permits it and the need for repair or replacement is caused by misuse by the tenant, his family, or a guest (§ 92.162).

The landlord may require advance payment if the lease permits it and either the tenant is more then thirty days delinquent in paying for the last repair or replacement or the last repair or replacement was done less than thirty days ago (§ 92.162).

If the landlord requires payment, a reasonable time is seven days from the date prepayment is received (§ 92.161).

However, if during the last two months a break-in occurred or was attempted in the rental unit or complex or a crime of personal violence occurred, then a reasonable time is only seventy-two hours after the request or prepayment.

If the landlord fails to install or rekey the security devices required by this law, the tenant can rekey or repair herself and deduct the rent, terminate the lease, or file suit. To terminate the lease, she must give the landlord a written request and three days to comply. The landlord gets seven days if his written lease contains notices underlined or in boldface print regarding the landlord's duty to install security devices and the tenant's right to install or rekey and deduct the cost from is rent. This additional time applies only if there have been no break-ins, no attempted break-ins, or crimes of personal violence at the unit or complex within the last two months (§§ 92.164 and 92.165).

The tenant must give the landlord notice of any rent reduction for making the repairs herself and give the landlord a duplicate upon written request (§ 92.167).

The tenant can sue the management company for failure to install or repair security devices. But the management company will not be liable if it can prove that the owner did not give it enough funds after written request to provide funds for such installation or repair, and the management company gives the tenant notice within three days after receiving the tenant's notice that it does not have the funds and made written request to the owner for the funds. If the management company gives a tenant this notice, the tenant may terminate the lease, fix the security device and reduce rent for the cost of repair, or sue the landlord (§§ 92.167 and 92.168).

SMOKE DETECTORS

Each residential leased dwelling must have a working smoke detector installed outside, but near, each bedroom. If the unit uses a single room for dining, living, and sleeping, the detector must be in that room. If a bedroom is upstairs, the detector must be on the ceiling directly above the top of the stairway. If the bedrooms are served by the same hall or corridor, one smoke detector must be in the corridor in the immediate vicinity of the bedrooms. The smoke detector must be installed on a ceiling or wall at least six inches but no further than twelve inches from the ceiling unless some other location is approved by ordinance or the local fire marshal (§ 92.251, et seq.).

It must detect both visible and invisible combustion products; be audible to the bedrooms it serves; be powered by a battery, AC current, or other power source as specified by local ordinance; and must be tested and approved by Underwriters Laboratories, Factory Mutual Research Corp., or U.S. Testing Company.

While the landlord must make sure the smoke detector is working at the beginning if the lease term, subsequent inspection or repair is required only after a request from the tenant. Replacement batteries are a tenant's responsibility. Inspection means using the manufacturer's testing procedures.

The lease can require the tenant to make written request for inspection or repair. If the repair is needed because of damages caused by a tenant or guest, the landlord can require the tenant to pay the repair costs before making the repair.

If the landlord fails to install, inspect, or repair a smoke detector as required, and the tenant gives the landlord written seven days notice, the tenant can terminate the lease and sue for damages, attorney's fees, and a penalty of one month's rent plus $100. In order to exercise these remedies, the tenant must be current on rent, and must have paid in advance for the repairs if required by the landlord [see § 92.258(C)].

If the tenant removes the battery without replacing it with a working one, or otherwise disables a smoke detector, the landlord can sue for damages. If the lease contains an underlined or bold-type notice telling the tenant not to disconnect the smoke detector or remove the battery, the landlord can sue for a penalty of one month's rent plus $100, attorney's fees, and court costs if the tenant disconnects or fails to replace the battery within seven days after the landlord gives the tenant written notice to reconnect or repair. The obvious purpose of this law is to make landlords install smoke detectors to prevent injury and death from fires. If the landlord doesn't have a working smoke detector and tenant is killed or injured, the landlord pays.

The parties cannot waive the rights and duties provided by this section, except that they can waive, by written agreement, the landlord's duty to inspect and repair the smoke detector, as long as one is installed and working at the time the lease begins (§ 92.006).

CODE VIOLATIONS

Landlords should be aware that governmental bodies can levy fines of hundreds of dollars a day for minor violations. Ignoring notices of violation can be expensive. Whenever you receive a governmental notice you should read it very carefully and follow it to the letter. After you correct a violation, be sure that the governmental body which sent the notice gives you written confirmation that you are in compliance.

WARRANTY OF HABITABILITY

Under Texas case law, there was an "implied warranty of habitability" in a residential lease. However, in passing Chapter 92 of the Property Code, the legislature made the rights and duties under Chapter 92 for residential tenancies to be in lieu of (instead of) any common law rights or warranties regarding habitability, repair, maintenance, security, etc. (see § 92.061).

LANDLORD LIABILITY 5

The law of responsibilities for injuries and crime on rental property has changed considerably over the last couple decades. The law which held for hundreds of years that landlords are not liable was overturned and landlords are now often liable, even for conditions that are not their fault. This change was not made by elected legislators representing their constituents, but by appointed judges who felt tenants needed protection and landlords should give it to them.

INJURIES ON THE PREMISES

AREAS UNDER LANDLORD'S CONTROL

The landlord has a duty to inspect and repair common areas in a rental building with more than one unit. This duty does not apply to a single family home, since the entire premises is under the tenant's control.

AREAS NOT UNDER THE LANDLORD'S CONTROL

The general rule is that a landlord is not liable for injuries on parts of the premises that are not under his or her control except in the following circumstances:

- ☞ Where there is a danger known to the landlord
- ☞ Where there is a violation of law in the condition of the premises caused by the landlord

☞ Where the landlord undertakes to repair the premises or is required by the lease to do the repairs, and the dangerous condition is created by the repairs

☞ Where the landlord did a negligent act

Landlord's Warranty of Habitability

Under Texas case law, there was an implied warranty of habitability in a residential lease. However, in passing Chapter 92 of the Property Code, the legislature made the rights and duties under Chapter 92 in lieu of (instead of) any common law rights or warranties regarding habitability, repair, maintenance, security, etc. (§ 92.061).

Protection from Liability for Injuries

The basis for liability in these cases is that the landlord breached a duty to keep the premises safe. If a landlord puts the duty to keep the premises safe on the tenant, there will be less likelihood that the landlord can be held liable. Property Code, Section 92, allows a landlord to put certain duties of maintenance on the tenant in a single-family dwelling or duplex. (See chapter 2.) A non-residential lease can do the same. But in a multi-family building, the landlord cannot get out of the burden of making sure the part of the premises under his or her possession and control are reasonably safe at all times.

A landlord cannot immunize himself or herself against liability for his or her own negligent actions. The landlord is not the insurer or guarantor of the safety of tenants but must only use reasonable care to keep the areas under his control in a safe condition. However, he or she should carry adequate insurance to cover any liability. This means that rents should be raised accordingly to cover this insurance.

CRIMES AGAINST TENANTS

Another area where liability of landlords has been greatly expanded is in the area of crimes against tenants. The former theory of law was that a person cannot be held liable for deliberate acts of third parties. This had been the theory for hundreds of years but has recently been abandoned in favor of a theory that a landlord must protect tenants from crimes.

The theory has been stated to be that where the landlord can foresee the possibility of criminal attack, the landlord must take precautions to prevent it. But some have said that this means that any time an attack is possible, the landlord must protect the tenant. This would include nearly every tenancy, especially in urban areas. New Jersey has gone so far as to hold landlords strictly liable for every crime committed on their property whether or not they knew there was a risk or took any precautions. This liability for crime applies to both residential and commercial tenancies, but it has not been extended to single-family homes—yet.

📖 In one case, a jury found a landlord liable for the tenant's damages when she was raped by an intruder because the landlord knew for a long time that the locks on the tenant's windows were broken, but refused to install working locks (as required by Chapter 92 of the Property Code), and was aware that the complex was in a high crime area and that there had been previous instances of criminal activity in the complex.

📖 In another case in Texas, a woman was awarded $17 million when she was raped by someone who broke into the management office and stole apartment keys. She had previously asked for a lock which could not be opened from the outside, but the management refused, saying they needed access to all units.

📖 In a recent case from Houston, the appellate court upheld a $344,000 judgment against an apartment complex, in favor of a rape victim. The court said that the crime history of the complex created a foreseeable unreasonable risk of violent activity that could probably have been prevented with a controlled access gate, perimeter fencing, and a night security guard. *Dickin Arms-Reo, L.P. v. Campbell*, (Case No.01-97-01190-CV; 9/23/99 Houston).

PROTECTION FROM LIABILITY FOR CRIMES

The law is not clear in Texas as to just how far courts will go in holding landlords liable for crimes against tenants. A clause in a lease that makes a tenant responsible for locks and security may provide some protection to landlords in some situations, especially in single-family homes and duplexes.

In some inner-city apartment complexes where crime is common, landlords may be required to provide armed guards or face liability. Again, insurance is a must and this additional cost will have to be covered by rent increases. Isn't it interesting that homeowners cannot get insurance from crimes such as rape, but that tenants get free insurance out of the landlord's pocket?

CRIMES BY TENANTS AGAINST NONTENANTS

In one case where a commercial tenant was selling counterfeit goods with such trademarks as Rolex and Polo, a United States District Court held that the landlords could be held liable if they knew of the activities of the tenants and did nothing to stop them. *Polo Ralph Lauren Corp. v. Chinatown Gift Shop*, 93 CIV 6783 TPG (United States District Court for the Southern District of New York, June 21, 1994).

CHANGING THE TERMS OF THE TENANCY 6

ASSIGNMENT OR SUBLEASE BY TENANT

Under Property Code, § 91.005, a tenant is prohibited from assigning his or her lease to someone else, and from subletting all or a portion of the premises unless the landlord gives prior permission. A written lease can permit assignment or subletting without prior consent, but if the lease is silent, the above law controls.

ASSIGNMENT   An *assignment* is where a tenant assigns all of her interest in a lease to another party who takes over the tenant's position. The original tenant is called the *assignor* and the new tenant is called the *assignee*.

SUBLEASE   A *sublease* is where the tenant enters into a new agreement with a third party who deals solely with the tenant. The original tenant is then called the *sublessor* and the new tenant is called the *sublessee*.

LIABILITY   If a lease contains a covenant to pay rent and the landlord does not release the tenant from this obligation upon the assignment, the landlord may still sue the original tenant if the new tenant defaults.

WAIVER   If a landlord knowingly accepts rent from an assignee or a sublessee of a lease, the landlord waives the right to object to the assignment. But, if the landlord was unaware of the assignment, it does not constitute a waiver.

Notice of Rule Change

If the landlord changes rules or policies regarding tenant's personal property, such as parking policies, the landlord must give prior written notice of such change to his or her tenants. Tenants must be notified either by mail, personal delivery, or attaching the notice to the inside of the main entry door (§ 92.013).

Closing the Rental Premises

Under § 92.055, even if the lease term is not complete, a landlord can close a rental premises at any time by using the following procedure:

First, the landlord must give written notice to by certified mail, return receipt requested, to the tenant, the local health officer, and the local building inspector stating that:

☛ the landlord is terminating the tenancy as soon as legally possible; and

☛ after the tenant moves out, the landlord will either demolish the unit or no longer use it for residential purposes.

After the tenant moves out of the premises, the local health officer or building inspector may not allow occupancy until he or she certifies that there is no known adverse health or safety condition. The landlord cannot permit reoccupancy for six months.

If the landlord gives the closing notice after receiving a repair notice provided in § 92.052, and the tenant moves out on or before the end of the lease term, the landlord must pay the tenant's reasonable moving expenses, give the tenant a prorate refund of rent, and refund the security deposit. The tenant can also sue the landlord for actual damages, a penalty of one month's rent plus $500, attorney's fees, and court costs.

Obviously then, unless there is a serious health or safety problem, a landlord will not use this procedure to close a unit. He'll just wait until the lease term ends, give the tenant notice that he won't renew the lease, and then quietly close the unit.

SALE OF PROPERTY BY LANDLORD

A landlord has the right to sell property covered by a lease, but the new owner takes the property subject to the terms of the existing leases. The new owner cannot cancel the old leases or raise the rent while the leases are in effect (unless the lease provisions allow the landlord to do so).

The new owner must make any repairs to the property that the old owner would have had to do under the terms of the lease. In most cases, the old landlord is relieved of his or her obligations under a lease upon sale of the property.

When selling property, a landlord must specify in the sales contract that the sale is subject to existing leases. Otherwise the buyer may sue for failure to deliver the premises free and clear of encumbrances. At closing, the leases should be assigned to the buyer.

FORECLOSURES When property is purchased at a foreclosure sale, the leases of the tenants are terminated if they were signed after the date of the mortgage. A mortgage holder will sometimes agree that a foreclosure does not terminate the lease.

RAISING THE RENT

If a tenancy is for a set term (such as a one year lease) at a specified rent, the landlord cannot raise the rent until the term ends unless such a right is spelled out in the lease. If the tenancy is month-to-month (or for a lesser period, such as week-to-week), the landlord can raise the rent if he gives notice equal to the rent paying period (§ 91.001). That is, for a month-to-month tenancy, notice must be given at least thirty days prior to the end of the month; and for a week-to-week tenancy, notice must be given at least one week in advance. To raise the rent in a month-to-month tenancy you can use form 9.

In such a case, the tenant would probably not have to give thirty days notice if she decided not to stay at the end of the month. This is because by raising the rent the landlord would be terminating the previous tenancy and making the tenant an offer to enter into a new tenancy at a different rental rate.

Modifying the Lease

If you agree to modify the terms of your lease with a tenant you should put it in writing. If you do not and you allow a tenant to do things forbidden in the lease you may be found to have waived your rights. A simple modification form is included in this book as form 30.

PROBLEMS DURING THE TENANCY 7

VIOLATIONS BY THE TENANT

VACATING EARLY

If the tenant breaches the lease by vacating the property before the expiration of the lease, the landlord may do one of three things: 1) Terminate the lease and take possession of the property for the landlord's own account (relieving the tenant of further liability); 2) Take possession of the premises for the account of the tenant and hold the tenant liable for the difference in rent due under the lease and the rent eventually received; 3) Take possession for the account of the tenant, re-rent the premises and sue the old tenant for the difference between the rent due under the old lease and the rent received from the new tenant. Under Section 91.000 of the Texas Property Code, enacted in 1997, a landlord has a duty to mitigate damages if the tenant abandons the premises in violation of the lease. In other words, the landlord has a duty to try to re-rent the premises for the best market rent. Section 91.006 voids any lease provision that tries to waive this duty.

The law in this area is very complicated. Also, the parties may, in their lease agreement, agree to remedies different from the "common law" rules described above. Before taking action regarding large sums of money, a landlord should consult an attorney.

Problems. When a landlord evicts a tenant, this terminates the lease and precludes suit for future rent. Also,when a landlord's actions or words constitute a forfeiture of the lease, the tenant won't be liable for damages or future rents. Therefore, the landlord needs to be careful so there will be no misrepresentation or misunderstanding of his intent. The landlord should not use the word "forfeited" in any correspondence with the tenant or in his complaint filed with the court.

Possible Solutions. The usual problem in the court cases is a misinterpretation of the landlord's intent. To avoid this, the landlord should analyze his or her options and make his of her intent clear either in the form of a certified letter to the tenant or in the allegations of the complaint.

BAD CHECKS   Under Texas Statutes, Article 90222, a holder of a bad check can charge a service charge of $25. The procedure is to send a notice by certified mail and then file suit on the check. However, if a tenant cannot immediately make good on a check, the landlord would be better advised to immediately start the eviction rather than sue on the bad check.

There is also a criminal law against writing a bad check and this is Texas Penal Code, § 32.41. Usually, your District Attorney has a hot check division which may prosecute the tenant. However, you must comply with certain requirements, such as checking the identification of the maker of the check and not taking a post-dated check.

VIOLATIONS BY THE LANDLORD

RETALIATORY
CONDUCT   Under sections 92.331 and 92.332, the landlord cannot retaliate against a tenant for exercising a tenant's right under the lease, law, or ordinance; giving notice to repair; or complaining to a governmental entity by evicting, decreasing services, depriving the tenant of possession, increasing rent, or terminating the lease. However, it is not retaliation if the landlord evicts for delinquent rent, intentional damage by the tenant, threatening words or conduct, material breach, holding over after giving notice to terminate, holding over after the end of the lease term and the

landlord gives notice of termination before receiving a notice to repair, or holding over after the landlord's termination notice given based on a good faith belief that the tenant will damage the property, or adversely affect the other tenants or neighbors.

If the landlord retaliates, the tenant can sue and recover one month's rent plus $500, actual damages, moving costs, attorney's fees, and court costs. If the tenant files suit in bad faith, the landlord can recover a penalty of one month's rent plus $500, attorney's fees, and court costs. Landlord retaliation is also a defense to an eviction suit, and rent lawfully withheld is a defense for nonpayment of rent (§ 92.335).

If a tenant withholds or deducts rent or makes repairs in violation of this statute, the landlord can sue the tenant after giving him written notice of the illegality of what he is doing and the possible penalties. If the landlord wins, he can win a judgment for actual damages. If, after receiving the notice, and the tenant keeps withholding or deducting rent, or making repairs in bad faith, the landlord can also recover one month's rent plus $500 as a penalty (§ 92.058).

INTERRUPTING UTILITIES

A landlord cannot interrupt utility service paid for directly by the tenant to the utility company except for repairs, construction, or emergencies (§ 92.008).

If the landlord is required by the lease to furnish utilities (water, gas, or electricity), and any of the utilities are cut off or threatened to be cut off because the landlord failed to pay the bill, the tenant has the following remedies (§ 92.301):

☛ Pay the bill and deduct the amount from rent due

☛ Terminate the lease and deduct the security deposit from the rent due

☛ Terminate the lease and get a pro rata refund of any prepaid rent

☛ Sue for damages including moving costs, storage fees, lost wages, utility connect fees, attorney's fees

If the landlord can provide to the tenant evidence that the bill has been paid before the tenant moves out or sues, the tenant's right to move out or sue stops. The parties cannot waive these rights and duties (92.006).

A commercial landlord cannot interrupt or cutoff utilities paid for directly by tenant except for repairs, construction, or emergencies. That means if the landlord pays the utilities, he can cutoff a commercial tenant who doesn't pay the rent.

RESIDENTIAL
LOCK OUT OR
REMOVAL OF
PROPERTY

A landlord may not lock out or otherwise prevent a tenant from entering the premises without a court order unless for repairs, construction, or emergencies, removal of abandoned property, or changing door locks of a delinquent tenant. Before locks can be changed for delinquent rent, the landlord must mail, five days in advance, or post inside the main entry door, three days in advance, a notice of the earliest date the landlord intends to change the locks, the amount of delinquent rent, and the name and address of the person or a location of on site office where the rent may be paid during normal business hours.

If locks are changed, the landlord must place written notice on the tenant's front door stating (a) an on-site location where the tenant may get a key twenty-four hours a day, or a telephone number that the tenant may call to get a key within two hours; (b) that the landlord must give the tenant a key even if he doesn't pay the back rent; and (c) the amount of back rent and other charges. The landlord can't change the locks and leave town or otherwise be unavailable. If the landlord shows up with a new key in a timely manner and the tenant is not present, the landlord must leave another notice stating when the landlord arrived and where the tenant can go to get the key during normal office hours.

If a landlord locks out a tenant without following these procedures, a tenant must file suit in justice court for a writ of reentry. The landlord is entitled to a hearing (§ 92.009). The rights of the tenant and obligations of the landlord under the lock out statute cannot be waived. A tenant can recover the greater of $500 or his actual damages, less any delinquent rent, plus attorney's fees and court costs.

The following cases from other states show what can happen:

📖 In a Missouri case, a landlord took the refrigerator, washing machine, and stove because the tenant failed to pay rent and the tenant was awarded $10,000 in damages. *Smiley v. Cardin*, 655 S.W.2d 114 (Mo.Ct.App. 1983).

📖 In a District of Columbia case where purchasers of a tax deed to property kept changing the locks on the property, nailing the door shut, and nailing "for sale" signs on the property when the occupant was away, a jury awarded the occupant $250,000 in punitive damages. They had used those tactics to try to force the occupant to sue them so that the government would have to defend their tax deed. The appeals court upheld the verdict. *Robinson v. Sarisky*, 535 A.2d 901 (D.C.App. 1988).

📖 In a Florida case, a landlord posted a three-day notice and when the tenant was absent from the premises, he entered and removed her possessions. She testified in a lawsuit that her possessions were all heirlooms and antiques and since the landlord had disposed of them, he could not prove otherwise. She was awarded $31,000 in damages. *Reynolds v. Towne Mgt. of Fla., Inc.*, 426 So.2d 1011 (Fla. 2 DCA 1983).

A commercial landlord may not prevent a tenant from entering the leases premises except for repairs, construction, emergency, to remove abandoned property, or for failure to pay rent on time. If the tenant is delinquent in paying rent, the landlord may change the locks and must give notice on the tenant's front door of where and from whom a new key can be obtained. The new key only has to be given to the tenant during the tenant's regular business hours and only if tenant first pays the rent current (§ 93.002).

If the landlord violates this law, the tenant can sue for the greater of the tenant's actual damage, one month's rent or $500. The tenant can also sue to recover possession of the leased premises by filing a complaint for reentry in justice court (§ 93.003).

A commercial landlord cannot remove doors, windows, locks, door-knobs, etc. or furniture, fixtures, appliances furnished by the landlord except for repair or replacement (§ 93.002).

DESTRUCTION OF THE PREMISES

If the premises are damaged by fire, smoke, hail, tornado, hurricane, or other such event, it does not necessarily automatically terminate the lease. If the premises are totally unusable for residential purposes, and the loss is not the fault of the tenant, or the tenant's family or guest, either party may terminate the lease by written notice to the other. This notice may be given at any time before repairs are completed. If the lease is terminated in this manner, the tenant is entitled to a prorated refund of rent, from the date of moving out, and a refund of any security deposit.

If the premises are partially unusable and the loss is not caused by the tenant, or the tenant's family or guest, the tenant is entitled to a reduced rent. However, unless the parties reach an agreement on the reduced rent amount or it is otherwise provided for in the lease, the tenant will need to file suit to have the court determine the amount of reduced rent to be paid.

If the damages are covered by insurance, the landlord's repair period does not begin until insurance proceeds are received.

PROBLEMS AT THE END OF THE TENANCY

8

TENANT HOLDING OVER

Where the tenant holds over at the end of a lease, the landlord has two options:

1. Treat the tenant as a trespasser and demand and sue for possession and damages, based on the reasonable rental value of the premises, demand double rent and possession of the property.

2. Treat the tenancy as continuing under the original lease.

Under the second option, the landlord is entitled to the rental rate under the original lease. The landlord and tenant can agree in the lease that if the landlord permits a holdover, the rent will be increased by a specific amount or percentage.

DAMAGE TO THE PREMISES

If the landlord finds damage at the end of a tenancy, then he may deduct the amount of the damage from the security deposit. In a residential tenancy, the landlord forfeits that right if he does not send the correct notice within fifteen days of when the tenant vacates the premises. (See chapter 3.)

If the damages exceed the amount of the security deposit, the landlord may sue the tenant. If the damages are under $5,000, the landlord can file the case in small claims court.

PROPERTY ABANDONED BY TENANT

COMMERCIAL

A landlord may remove and store any property left by a tenant who has abandoned the premises. If the property is unclaimed for sixty days, the landlord may dispose of it, but must first give the tenant notice by certified mail that the landlord may dispose of the property if not claimed within sixty days (§ 93.002).

RESIDENTIAL

A residential landlord may remove the contents of a leased premises the tenant has abandoned. See chapter 11 for more information about seizing a tenant's property as compensation for unpaid rent or damages to the premises.

MUNICIPAL UTILITY SERVICE LIENS

Some municipalities have attempted in the past to hold landlords hostage for tenants' unpaid utility bills by placing liens on the property by requiring the landlord to guarantee the bill or by refusing service to a new tenant until the landlord pays the old bill. To prevent such abuse, the legislature passed a law which prohibits a municipality from requiring payment of a previous customer's bill as a condition of connecting a new customer and prohibits a municipality from requiring a third party to guarantee a utility bill. The law permits a lien for utility bills if the municipality passes an ordinance, and the property is not a homestead, but does not apply to a tenant's utility bill if the landlord notifies the municipality that the property is a rental property.

Terminating a Tenancy 9

Termination in General

A tenancy may be terminated in several ways. Unless the tenancy is terminated properly, the tenant may not be evicted. If you file an eviction without properly terminating the tenancy, the tenant may win the case and you may be ordered to pay damages to the tenant as well as the tenant's attorney fees.

A tenancy for a fixed term automatically terminates at the end of the specified term. When the term of the lease ends, the tenant is expected to vacate the property without notice. This is different from some states where a lease is presumed to be renewed unless one party gives the other notice. If you believe that a tenant may not be expecting to leave at the end of the lease, you may want to make sure the tenant is aware the lease is terminating by using form 10.

A periodic tenancy can be terminated at any time by giving a notice equal to the rental payment period (e.g., one month's notice if rent is paid monthly, or one week's notice if paid weekly); or whatever amount of notice the parties agree to in their lease. A tenancy at will may be terminated by either party at any time.

In addition to termination at the end of the term in a tenancy for a fixed term, or after notice in a periodic tenancy, a tenancy can be terminated by one of the following occurrences:

☞ The occurrence of a condition agreed to by the parties in the lease. The landlord and tenant can agree that a particular condition, such as sale of the property, destruction or condemnation of part of the property, etc., will cause the tenancy to be terminated.

☞ Condemnation (taking for government purposes) of all of the property by a governmental authority automatically terminates a lease.

☞ Breach by the landlord or tenant of certain terms of the lease which the parties have agreed will constitute termination.

☞ Abandonment of the premises can cause a termination if the landlord accepts the abandonment as a termination. This is discussed in more detail in the section in this chapter on "Early Termination by Tenant."

☞ Closing of the residential premises by a landlord after receipt of a demand to repair. This is discussed in more detail in chapter 2.

☞ Termination by tenant of a residential lease for failure of the landlord to make certain repairs or install security devices or smoke detectors. This is discussed in more detail in chapter 2.

The death of the landlord or tenant does not terminate a lease, unless the parties agree that such death would end their lease.

Early Termination by Tenant

REMEDIES FOR
BREACH

If the tenant breaches the lease by vacating early, the landlord has four options:

1. Declare the lease forfeited and take possession of the premises for the landlord's own account (this relieves the tenant of liability for

further rent). This will be the best option if you can easily rent the unit at a higher rental rate.

2. Take possession of the premises and sue for the difference between the present value of the contractual rent and the reasonable market value of the lease for the rest of the term. From a practical standpoint, this is very similar to option 3 below.

3. Take possession of the premises for the account of the tenant, re-rent the premises, and then sue the old tenant for the difference between the rent due under the old lease and the rent received from the new tenant. If you expect to rent the unit at a lower rate, you should make it clear that you are taking possession for the tenant's account. From a practical standpoint, this is very similar to option 2 above.

4. Allow the premises to sit vacant and sue the tenant for the rent as it becomes due. This option may be best if the landlord has many vacant units.

While you have no legal duty to try to relet in order to mitigate damages, in most cases, unless you or the tenant just won the lottery, you should try to relet as the surest way to minimize your loss.

The law in this area is very complicated. Also, the parties may, in the lease, agree to remedies different from the common law rules described above. Before taking action regarding large sums of money, you should consult a lawyer.

When a landlord's actions or words constitute a forfeiture of the lease, the tenant won't be liable for damages or future rents. Therefore, the landlord needs to be careful so there will be no misrepresentation of his or her intent. The landlord should not use the word "forfeit" in any correspondence with the tenant, or in a complaint (petition?) filed with the court.

Early Termination of Residential Tenancy by Landlord

A landlord may terminate a tenancy before the end of the term for two reasons: nonpayment of rent or a breach of the lease other than the nonpayment of rent.

The laws are very strict about terminating a tenancy and if they are not followed, the landlord may lose the case and be required to pay the tenant damages and attorney's fees. Be sure to read all of the following instructions carefully and follow them exactly.

Under Texas law, when a tenant refuses to surrender possession of the premises after demand, and is in default of paying rent or holding over after termination of the right to possession, he has committed what is called a *forcible detainer*. You may hear the term "forcible entry and detainer" used in connection with eviction of a tenant, but this phrase is technically incorrect. However, since most non-lawyers aren't aware of the distinction, don't worry about it, just follow these procedures (Property Code, Chapter 24).

NOTICE TO VACATE

First, the landlord must make written demand to vacate, called a "Notice to Vacate Prior to Filing Eviction Suit." This notice must give the tenant at least three days to vacate the premises before the landlord can sue to evict unless the parties have, in a written lease, agreed to a shorter or longer notice period. If the tenant is holding over beyond the end of the lease term, the landlord must first have given any notice required by Section 91.001 of the Property Code (see appendix A for selected sections).

The notice to vacate must either be given to the tenant in person, or sent by mail to the tenant at the leased premises. Notice in person is by any of the following methods:

☛ Personal delivery to the tenant

☛ Personal delivery to anyone sixteen years old or over residing at the premises

☞ Posting the notice inside the main entry

☞ If there is a mailbox, and a deadbolt, alarm system, or dangerous animal (i.e., doberman) which prevents entrance into the premises and placement of the notice on the inside of the front door, you may securely affix the notice to the outside of the main entry door.

Notice by mail must be either by regular mail or by certified mail, return receipt requested. The three day notice period begins on the day the notice is delivered to the premises (§ 24.005). Form 15, 17, or 18 in appendix C can be used for this purpose.

If you have given the tenant a written notice or reminder that rent is past due, your notice to vacate may include a demand that the tenant either pay the rent current or vacate the premises.

If the landlord wants to hire an attorney to file the eviction suit, and sue for attorney's fees, the tenant must be given notice ten days before filing suit. This notice must be sent by certified mail, return receipt requested; and it must inform the tenant that if he or she doesn't vacate before the eleventh day after receipt of the notice, the landlord will file suit and may recover attorney's fees. This ten day notice is not required if the written lease permits the recovery of attorney's fees. A Notice to Vacate (form 16) giving the ten day notice is included in appendix C.

The following are some common problems that can occur:

☞ **Amount Due.** The notice should only include amounts due for rent, not late charges or utility bills. If the lease clearly states that late charges are part of the "rent," you may get away with including them.

☞ **Attempts to Pay.** If a tenant attempts to pay the rent before the three day notice is up, the landlord must accept it. If the landlord wants to evict the tenant anyway, the only way to do it is if the tenant violates another clause in the lease. If the tenant attempts to pay the rent after the tenancy has been terminated (after the three days are up), the landlord does not have to accept it.

☛ **Acceptance of Rent.** If the landlord accepts rent with the knowledge that the tenant is not complying with some aspect of the lease, the landlord waives the right to evict for that noncompliance.

☛ **Undated Notice.** If a three day notice is not dated, it is invalid.

If the tenant does not move out within the three days, the next step is to file a suit for forcible detainer, which is explained in chapter 10.

PUBLIC AND SUBSIDIZED HOUSING

PUBLIC
HOUSING

For non-payment of rent, the landlord must give the tenant fourteen days notice rather than a three day notice and it must be mailed or hand delivered, not posted [24 CFR 866.4(1)(2)]. The notice must inform the tenant of his or her right to a grievance procedure.

At least one court has held that both a fourteen-day notice under the Federal regulation and a three-day notice under state law must be given. *Stanton v. Housing Authority of Pittsburgh*, 469 F.Supp. 1013 (W.D.Pa.1977). However, other courts have disagreed. *Ferguson v. Housing Authority of Middleboro*, 499 F.Supp. 334 (E.D.Ky 1980). One Florida court held that posting both a fourteen day notice and a three day notice is too confusing. It suggested that the landlord only use a fourteen day notice or else deliver the three day notice so that the deadline was the same as for the fourteen day notice. *Broward Co. Housing Authority v. Simmons*, 4 F.L.W.Supp. 494 (Co.Ct. Broward 1996).

📖 The public housing authority must prove both that the tenant did not pay the rent and that the tenant was at fault for not paying it. *Maxton Housing Authority v. McLean*, 328 S.E.2d (N.C. 1985).

📖 A Louisiana court held that a tenant was not at fault because her former husband did not pay the child support. *Housing Authority of City of New Iberia v. Austin*, 478 So.2d 1012 (La.App. 1986) writ denied, 481 So.2d 1334 (La. 1986). (Did they think that it was the landlord's fault?)

SECTION 236
APARTMENTS

For breach of the terms of the lease other than payment of rent, a thirty-day notice must be given, except in emergencies, and it must inform the tenant of the reasons for termination, her right to reply, and her right to a grievance procedure [24 CPR 366(4)(1)]. If the tenant requests a grievance hearing, a second notice must be given, even if the tenant loses in the hearing. *Ferguson v. Housing Authority of Middleboro*, 499 F.Supp. 432 (E.D.Ky. 1980).

For nonpayment of rent, tenants must be given the three-day notice and be advised that if there is a judicial proceeding, they can present a valid defense, if any. Service must be by first class mail and hand delivered or placed under the door [24 CFR 450.4(a)].

For breach of the terms of the lease other than payment of rent, the tenant must first have been given notice that in the future such conduct would be grounds for terminating the lease. The notice of termination must state when the tenancy will be terminated, specifically why it is being terminated, and it must advise the tenant of the right to present a defense in the eviction suit (24 CFR 450).

SECTION 8
APARTMENTS

Under 24 CFR 882.215(c)(4), the landlord must notify the housing authority in writing at the commencement of the eviction proceedings. Also, the previous paragraph on acceptance of rent and waiver applies to Section 8 housing as well.

DEATH OF A TENANT

The death of a tenant does not terminate the tenancy. The tenant's estate is responsible for fulfilling the terms of the lease. A landlord can request, in writing, that the tenant (a) give landlord the name, address, and telephone number of a person to contact if the tenant dies; and (b) authorize the landlord to permit such person access to remove personal property and receive any security deposit refund. If after written notice is mailed to the designated person by certified mail, return receipt requested, no one picks up the property within thirty days, the landlord may discard it.

EVICTING A TENANT 10

The only way a landlord may recover possession of a dwelling unit is if the tenant abandons it or voluntarily surrenders it to the landlord, or if the landlord gets a court order giving the landlord possession. As explained in chapter 7, self-help methods such as shutting off electricity or changing locks can result in thousands of dollars in fines. Fortunately, the eviction process usually works quite quickly in Texas. In some cases, tenants' lawyers have abused the system and allowed non-paying tenants to remain in possession for months, but most of the time, the system allows delinquent tenants to be removed quickly.

Before beginning an eviction case, be sure to read the subsection in chapter 7 on "Retaliatory Conduct."

SURRENDER OR ABANDONMENT

To surrender a dwelling, a tenant must tell the landlord that he or she is leaving or leave the keys. It can be presumed that a tenant abandoned the dwelling if the tenant has been absent for half of the rental term (unless the rent is current or notice is given).

Note: In some cases, such as where all of a tenant's possessions are gone and the electricity has been turned off at the direction of the tenant, a landlord would probably be safe in assuming abandonment; but in the unlikely event that a dispute went to court, the landlord could lose.

📖 In a Florida case, a landlord changed the locks the day after a lease expired. The tenant had moved most of his things out and had the utilities shut off. When the tenant sued saying he left a valuable Rolex on the premises, he lost. *Newman v. Gray*, 4 F.L.W. Supp. 271 (CC 11th Cir. Dade 1996).

SETTLING WITH THE TENANT

Although in a great majority of Texas evictions the tenants do not answer the complaint and the landlord wins quickly, some tenants can create nightmares for landlords. Clever tenants and legal aid lawyers can delay a case for months, and vindictive tenants can destroy the property with little worry of ever paying for it. Therefore, in some cases, lawyers advise their clients to offer the tenant a cash settlement to leave. For example, a tenant may be offered $200 to be out of the premises and leave it clean within a week. Of course, it hurts to give money to a tenant who already owes you money, but it could be cheaper than the court costs, vacancy time, and damages to the premises. Then again, an old American saying is, "Millions for defense but not one cent for tribute." You'll have to make your own decision based upon your tenant.

GROUNDS FOR EVICTION

A tenant can be evicted for nonpayment of rent, for violating one of the terms of the lease, for violating the Texas landlord/tenant law, or for failing to leave at the end of the lease. The most common violation of the lease is that the tenant has failed to pay the rent, but a tenant can also be evicted for violating other terms of the rental agreement, such as disturbing other tenants.

TERMINATING THE TENANCY

It is an ancient rule of law that an eviction suit cannot be filed until the tenancy is legally terminated. There are cases from the 1500s in which evictions were dismissed because the landlord failed to properly terminate the tenancy. If you make the same mistake, don't expect the judge to overlook it. What the judges often do is order the landlord to pay the tenant's attorney fees.

The tenancy may terminate by natural expiration or by action by the landlord. If you need to evict a tenant whose tenancy has not expired, you should carefully read the previous chapter and follow the procedures to properly terminate the tenancy.

USING AN ATTORNEY

The landlord/tenant statutes provide that the loser in a landlord/tenant case can be charged with the winner's attorney fees. Because of this, it is important to do an eviction carefully. In some cases, the tenant may just be waiting for the eviction notice before leaving the premises and in such a case the landlord may regain the premises no matter what kind of papers he files. But in other cases, tenants with no money and no defenses have gotten free lawyers, paid for by our tax dollars, who find technical defects in the case. This can cause a delay in the eviction and cause the landlord to be ordered to pay the tenant's attorney fees. A simple error in a landlord's court papers can cost him the case.

A landlord facing an eviction should consider the costs and benefits of using an attorney compared to doing it without an attorney. One possibility is to file the case without an attorney and hope the tenant moves. If the tenant stays and fights the case, an attorney can be hired to finish the case. Some landlords who prefer to do their evictions themselves start by paying a lawyer for a half-hour or hour of her time to review the facts of the case and point out problems. We know of some attorneys who loan this book to their clients and advise them as questions arise. Whenever a tenant has an attorney, the landlord should also have one.

It is, of course, important to find an attorney who both knows landlord/tenant law and charges reasonable fees. There are many subtleties of the law that can be missed by someone without experience. Some attorneys who specialize in landlord/tenant work charge very modest fees, such as $75 or $100, to file the case and the same amount for a short hearing, unless the case gets complicated. Others charge an hourly rate that can add up to thousands of dollars. You should check with other landlords or a local apartment association for names of good attorneys, or you might try calling the manager of a large apartment complex in the area.

If you get a security deposit at the beginning of the tenancy and start the eviction immediately upon a default, then the deposit should be nearly enough to cover a fair amount of the attorney's fee.

WHO CAN SUE?

In an eviction suit in justice court for nonpayment of rent or holding over, the parties may represent themselves or be represented by an authorized agent who need not be an attorney (§ 24.011; and Rule 747a, Rules of Civil Procedure). In any other type of eviction, you can represent yourself, but if you use a representative, he or she must be an attorney licensed to practice law in Texas. However, in any eviction suit in justice court where the tenant has not answered and you want to obtain a default judgment, you can use an authorized representative who need not be an attorney. These are exceptions to the general rule that only a licensed attorney may represent another person in court, which also applies to a corporation. In most lawsuits, not even a corporate officer can represent a corporation.

COURT PROCEDURES

The forcible detainer procedure is governed by the Civil Practices and Remedies Code, Chapter 24; and Rules 738 through 755 of the Rules of Civil Procedure. The case must be filed in the justice court (justice of the peace) in the precinct where the property is located. The clerk of the nearest justice court should be able to tell you in which precinct your property is located. Each justice court will usually have its own complaint form. The Sworn Complaint for Forcible Detainer (form 25 in appendix C) is based on the form used by Precinct No. 2 of Tarrant County.

You must put the following information in the petition:

☛ Name and full address of tenants, property address, and a service address if different from the property. Include all known home and work addresses.

☛ The date the lease was signed or the date the tenant moved into the property.

☛ The dates and amounts of rent due up to the day of filing, and a daily prorated rent amount (do not include late charges).

☛ The date of holdover if the suit is because of a holdover.

☛ The date you delivered to the tenant the notice to vacate.

☛ Your name, address, and telephone number.

As shown in the sample form, you can also sue for unpaid rent and attorney's fees up to $5,000 plus court costs (Rule 748).

Filing fees and service fees must be paid at the time the suit is filed. These fees change, and some courts may not accept personal checks, so call and ask first.

SERVICE OF PROCESS

Once the petition is filed, the clerk will prepare a *citation* and have the sheriff or constable serve (deliver it to) the tenant. Service (delivery) is made by the sheriff or constable by personal delivery of the petition and citation to the tenant/defendant or by leaving a copy of each of these documents with someone over sixteen years of age at the defendant's usual place of abode (Rule 742). If your sworn petition has listed all known home and work addresses and states that you know of no other home or work address in the county, the sheriff or constable can effect service by an alternative method. This involves the officer filing a sworn statement with the justice, and the justice ordering that service can be made by slipping the papers under the door or through the mail chute, or by affixing it (taping it) to the front door (Rule 742a). This type of service will support a default judgment for possession and unpaid rent (§ 24.0051).

DEFAULT
The tenant/defendant has six days to answer the lawsuit. If he or she does not answer by then, the court will issue a *default judgment*. If the tenant does answer, the court will set the case for trial and notify the landlord and tenant of date and time. The trial date will be set based on the court's schedule, usually within a week or two of service.

POSSESSION
BOND
The landlord has a way of getting the tenant out sooner than waiting until after trial. He can file a *possession bond* under Rule 740, Texas Rules of Civil Procedure. This bond can be filed at the time of filing the eviction suit or any time thereafter up until final judgment.

A possession bond is simply a promise by the landlord as principal, and one or more third parties as sureties, to pay for the tenant's damages if the court makes the tenant move out and the tenant later wins at trial. A *surety* is a person or company, usually an insurance company, who promises to pay those damages if the landlord doesn't. The surety will charge the landlord for this service. Some justices will accept personal sureties, like your attorney, but some will require corporate sureties (i.e., insurance companies). If you think you want to file a possession bond, call the clerk and ask for the judge's requirements on possession bonds.

Once a possession bond is approved and filed, the defendant will be given notice by the sheriff. The defendant has six days from receipt of the notice to do something, or the sheriff will move him or her out of the premises. Within the six days, the tenant/defendant must either:

- ☛ file a counterbond. This also must be approved by the justice and be in an amount set by the justice to cover the landlord's damages if he wins; or

- ☛ demand a trial be held before the six days are done.

If a trial is then held and the tenant loses, the sheriff will move him or her out of the premises five days after the trial. If a counterbond is filed, the tenant can stay in the property until the court rules at a later time that he or she loses.

Since the possession bond is expensive and difficult to obtain, and since it might subject the landlord to damages, unless you are afraid the tenant will destroy the premises or you think there will be a lengthy delay in getting a judgment, a possession bond might not be worth it for most residential properties.

JURY TRIAL   Either party may exercise their right to a jury trial, by requesting a jury within five days after service on the defendant and paying a $5 jury fee. As a landlord, you do not need or want a jury unless the justice in your precinct is biased in favor of tenants, which is unlikely. Either side can postpone the trial setting for up to six days, by filing a motion and affidavit showing good cause.

HEARING   The only issues in an eviction suit are: (1) who has the right to possession, and (2) the amount of the unpaid rent and attorney's fees if requested. Even if the tenant does not appear, the justice will make you prove your case. The difference is, if the tenant appears, there will probably be someone denying or contradicting everything you say. You should prepare your case thoroughly, even if you do not think the tenant will appear.

At trial, you will need to prove the following:

1. Existence of the lease or rental agreement. If the lease is written, show it to the justice. If it is oral, testify as to the date and

circumstances when the parties agreed, and the date the tenant moved into the unit. (***Note:*** Technically, whether the landlord owns the property is an issue. However, according to Rule 746, Rules of Civil Procedure, in an eviction suit, the tenant cannot contest ownership. This is called *estoppel to deny title of the landlord.* If the tenant tries to dispute your ownership, either in the eviction case or by filing another lawsuit in county court, you may need to get a lawyer).

2. Terms of the lease. If written, the lease will have the terms, but you need to tell the court the basics, such as amount of rent, date due, whether the lease is month to month or set term, etc.

3. The tenant's default or violation of the lease. If he has not paid rent as required, show the date of last payment; the dates payment was required but not made; any demands you made for payment; and the amount of rent due. Only include the unpaid, past due rent as of the trial date. Do not include any future rent or any late charges or penalties, just past due rent. If your lease provides that the tenant will pay you for utilities as additional rent, you can include this as well. You should bring your payment ledger. If the default is for something other than unpaid rent, you need to have sufficient evidence to show the default. If the tenant has held over beyond the end of term, id it's a periodic tenancy, have a copy of the notice to terminate required by § 91.001.

    If it's for another violation, have any necessary witness or document. (You can request the clerk to subpoena reluctant witnesses, but it must be done well in advance of the trial date and costs additional money.) Be prepared to fully explain how the tenant violated the lease. Justices are reluctant to throw a tenant out unless it is clear that he or she violated a material obligation of the lease such as paying rent.

4. That the lease gives the landlord the right to possession. When there is a written lease, it should be clear that a certain violation gives the landlord the right to possession. When the violation is unpaid rent, that is clear. Other violations are not so clear. Read the

lease. If it is still not clear, go see a lawyer. Some leases require the landlord to give notice of default to the tenant, who has a specified number of days to cure the default (like paying the past due rent). If you haven't given that required notice of default or didn't wait the stated number of days before delivering the notice to vacate, the justice of the peace will probably deny your eviction and you will have to start again.

5. Proper written notice to vacate. Be prepared to show the justice the written notice to vacate and to testify how and when it was delivered to the tenant or the premises. If you didn't deliver it, have the person who did come to court and testify. We recommend both personal delivery and certified mail, return receipt requested. If personal service was not done properly, or the tenant denies you gave notice, you have the certified mail green card or the returned letter as back up proof. (Getting the green card back usually takes a while, and the unclaimed certified letter takes a long time to come back, and might not be back by time of trial. Some justices may want to see the green card or unclaimed letter if the notice is disputed.)

6. Summarize. In summary, tell the justice precisely what you want, i.e., possession of the property, past due rent of x amount of dollars, and court costs. Make sure you figure out the rent due as of the trial date and give the judge that number. Things will go a lot easier of you make it easier for the justice.

> *Note:* Occasionally someone writes to us and says that they followed our book, but the justice gave the tenants extra time to move out, or in otherwise acted contrary to what we say here. Remember, usually a case will go smoothly, but justices do make mistakes. If your case gets complicated, you should find an experienced landlord/tenant attorney who can finish your case quickly.

Seeking Damages. More information about obtaining a money judgment against the tenant is contained later in this chapter. However, you should read that section before filing your eviction, since some of the forms in the eviction will be different.

Subsidized Housing. In Section 8 housing, the local housing authority must be notified in writing before the tenant can be served with the eviction [24 CFR 882.215(c)(4)].

If the tenant shows up with an attorney, and you were not told previously, you should ask the judge for a continuance to get your own attorney. If you make a mistake and lose, you may have to pay the tenant's attorney fees.

MONEY DAMAGES AND BACK RENT

Procedures for collecting money damages and back rent from a tenant are explained in the next chapter.

TENANT'S POSSIBLE DEFENSES

A tenant who is behind in rent usually has one objective—to stay in the property rent-free as long as possible. Tenants and the lawyers provided to them at no charge by legal aid clinics (paid for by landlords' tax dollars) sometimes come up with creative, though ridiculous, defenses. Here is case law to help defeat their arguments. But remember, the tenant should not be able to bring up any defenses unless she has paid the rent alleged to be due into the registry of the court.

CONSTITUTIONALITY   A tenant may claim it is unconstitutional to have a quick eviction procedure. The U.S. Supreme Court says that such procedures can be constitutional. *Lindsey v. Normet*, 465 US 56 (1972).

SECURITY
DEPOSIT   A tenant could say that he is not in default for nonpayment of rent because the landlord has his security deposit which covers the rent owed. This is not a defense because a security deposit is for a specific purpose at the end of the tenancy and does not cover current rent.

AMOUNT
INCORRECT

A tenant might dispute the amount of rent due. This is not a defense because if **any** rent is due then the landlord is entitled to eviction. However, if the amount stated in the three-day notice is wrong, the case could be dismissed.

TITLE

A tenant claims that the landlord has not proved he or she has good title to the property. A tenant who has entered into a rental agreement with a landlord is *estopped* (prohibited) from denying that the landlord has good title.

CORPORATION
IS DISSOLVED

Under Texas corporate law, a court action may not be maintained by a corporation which is not in good standing with the Texas Secretary of State. If your corporation has been dissolved, you should contact the Secretary of State to find out how to go about getting it reinstated. The Secretary of State may be contacted at:

Office of the Secretary of State
Corporations Section
P.O. Box 13697
Austin, TX 78711-3697
Tel. (512) 463-5555
Fax: (512) 463-5709
email: corpinfo.sos.state.tx.us/
http://www.state.tx.us

For more information about corporations in Texas, see *How to Form a Texas Corporation*, by Karen Ann Rolcik and Mark Warda, available through your local bookstore or directly from Sphinx Publishing by calling 1-800-226-5291.

WAIVER BY
REFUSAL TO
ACCEPT RENT

A tenant says that because the landlord refused the rent after the three days were up that it is a waiver of the rent. While the landlord does have to give the tenant three days to pay all past due rent, he does not have to accept rent after the three day period expires.

REGULATION Z

A tenant says that the landlord has not complied with Regulation Z (sometimes referred to simply as "Reg. Z") of the Code of Federal

Regulations. This is a truth-in-lending requirement, which does not apply to the rental of property [12 CFR 226.1(c)(1)].

UNCONSCIONABILITY OF RENT

A tenant claims that rent is unconscionable. This is a legal conclusion, and a tenant must state facts that would prove to the court that the rent is unconscionable.

INSUFFICIENT COMPLAINT

A tenant says that the landlord's petition is not drawn properly and does not state a cause of action. The petition forms included in this book include all elements necessary in a petition.

MAINTENANCE OF PREMISES

A tenant says that the landlord has not complied with the maintenance requirements of Chapter 92 of the Property Code, and that the tenant is withholding rent. This is not a valid defense unless certain requirements have been met. See the section on "Residential Tenancies" in chapter 4 for more details about notice and other requirements.

RETALIATORY CONDUCT

A tenant says that he is being evicted in retaliation for some lawful action. This defense does not apply if landlord is evicting the tenant for good cause such as non-payment of rent, violation of the lease or reasonable rules, or violation of the landlord/tenant law.

DISCOVERY

A tenant wants more time in order to take *discovery*, which means to ask questions of the landlord and any witnesses under oath before a court reporter. This should not delay the case for long. The discovery should be done quickly.

TENANT'S ATTORNEY BUSY OR UNPREPARED

The tenant's attorney may say that she just got on the case and needs time to prepare or has a busy schedule and is not available for trial for a month or so. This should not delay the case. The landlord has a right to a quick procedure. If the tenant's attorney is unavailable, he shouldn't have taken the case. Also, if the tenant has a lawyer, you should have one too.

GRIEVANCE PROCEDURE

In federally subsidized housing, the regulations require that tenants be given a grievance procedure in some evictions. However, where the tenant is a threat to the health and safety of other tenants or employees, Title 24 CFR, Chapter 9, §966.51(a) states such hearing is not required.

RENT PAYMENTS AFTER EVICTION BEGUN

Sometimes the tenant will want to pay rent after you've begun eviction to get you to stop. You want the money, but you also want the tenant out of the property. What can you do if past due rent is offered after notice to vacate or after eviction suit filed? You can accept rent and file or continue the eviction suit. While not necessary, your lease should have a clause that provides that acceptance of past due rent after notice to vacate does not waive your right to evict. In both such cases, you should make sure you inform the tenant that even though he has paid the back rent, you are proceeding with the eviction.

Note: Some justices will find that acceptance of past due rent waives your right to evict, even though that is not the law. You should check first before you accept.

Don't accept any payment that includes future rents unless you want to stop the eviction.

Sometimes the tenant will only have part of the past due rent. You want to give him a chance to stay, but don't want to waste the time, money, and effort you already spent in the eviction process. In this situation, you should require the tenant to sign an agreement that sets a payment schedule to bring the past due rent amount current and permits you to continue the eviction if he misses a payment.

JUDGMENT

After the trial, the justice will sign a judgment. If the tenant does not appear and you prove your case, the judge will sign a default judgment. If you win, it will be a judgment for possession, costs, and damages (rent). If the tenant wins, it will be a judgment for costs. Even if the tenant moves out of the premises before the trial, you can and should proceed with the case to get a judgment for possession and unpaid rent.

REGAINING POSSESSION

Once your Final Judgment has been signed by the justice, if the tenant has still not vacated the premises, you must take a Writ of Possession (the form is available from the court) and one extra copy of it to the clerk, and pay the sheriff or constable's fee for the eviction. The Writ of Possession orders the officer to:

☞ Deliver possession to the landlord

☞ Instruct the tenant to leave immediately and if he doesn't, to physically remove him

☞ Instruct the tenant to remove or allow the landlord or someone acting under the sheriff's authority, to remove all of the tenant's property

☞ Place the tenant's property outside, near the rental unit, but not on a sidewalk, passageway, or street and not while it's raining, sleeting, or snowing

☞ Post a warning on the tenant's door notifying her that the writ has been issued and will be executed on a certain date at least twenty-four hours after being posted

☞ The officer may, but is not required to, hire a bonded warehouse-man to remove and store the property, at no cost to the landlord or sheriff. If this happens, the warehouseman has a warehouseman's lien on the property and can sell it to collect the moving and storage fees (§ 24.0062). The tenant can get his property back by paying the moving and storage charges

Ask the clerk who executes the writ of possession in your precinct, the sheriff or constable, then call that office and find out the procedure. Some sheriffs will use a bonded warehouseman (moving company), while some will require you, the landlord, to hire the moving company. But they can't make you store the property. Usually, even the most stubborn deadbeat tenant will hightail it when he gets that notice from the sheriff.

If the personal property left on the premises appears to have been abandoned, then it should be treated as explained in chapter 8.

TENANT'S BANKRUPTCY

If a tenant files bankruptcy all legal actions against her must stop immediately. This provision is automatic from the moment the bankruptcy petition is filed (11 USC 362). If you take any action in court, seize the tenant's property, try to impose a landlord's lien or use the security deposit for unpaid rent, you can be held in contempt of federal court. It is not necessary that you receive formal notice. Verbal notice is sufficient. If you do not believe the tenant, then you should call the bankruptcy court to confirm the filing. The stay lasts until the debtor is discharged or the case is dismissed, or until the property is abandoned or voluntarily surrendered.

The landlord may ask for the right to continue with the eviction by filing a Motion for Relief from Stay and paying the filing fee (as of December, 1992, $60). Within thirty days a hearing is held and it may be held by telephone. The motion is governed by Bankruptcy Rule 9014 and the requirements of how the tenant must be served are contained in Rule 7004. However, for such a hearing the services of an attorney are usually necessary.

The bankruptcy stay only applies to amounts owed to the landlord at the time of filing the bankruptcy. The landlord can still sue the tenant for eviction and rent owed for any time period after the filing, unless the bankruptcy trustee assumes the lease. The landlord can proceed during the bankruptcy without asking for relief from the automatic stay under three conditions. *In re Knight*, 8 B.R. 925 (D.C. Md. 1981):

☛ The landlord can only sue for rent due after the filing

☛ The landlord cannot sue until the trustee rejects the lease. (If the trustee does not accept the lease within sixty days of the Order for Relief, then § 365(d)(1) provides that it is deemed rejected.)

☞ The landlord must sue under the terms of the lease and may not treat the trustee's rejection as a breach.

In a Chapter 13 reorganization bankruptcy, the landlord should be paid the rent as it comes due.

If the tenant filed bankruptcy after a judgment of eviction has been entered, there should be no problem lifting the automatic stay since the tenant has no interest in the property. *In re Cowboys, Inc.*, 24 B.R. (S.D. Fla. 1982).

If your tenant files bankruptcy and you decide it is worth hiring a lawyer, you should locate an attorney who is experienced in bankruptcy work. Prior to the meeting with the attorney, you should gather as much information as possible (type of bankruptcy filed, assets, liabilities, case number, etc.).

SATISFACTION OF JUDGMENT

If, after a judgment has been entered against the tenant, the tenant pays the amount due, it is the landlord's responsibility to file a Satisfaction of Judgment. A form may be obtained from the court.

COLLECTING MONEY FROM TENANTS 11

Trying to collect a judgment against a former tenant is usually not worth the time and expense. Most landlords are just glad to regain possession of the property. Tenants who don't pay rent usually don't own property that can be seized, and it is very difficult to garnish wages in Texas. However, occasionally former tenants come into money, and some landlords have been surprised many years later when called by a title insurance company wanting to pay off their judgment. Therefore, it is wise to include a claim for back rent in your eviction complaint.

In Texas, there are three types of statutory landlord's liens: the agricultural landlord's lien, the residential landlord's lien, and the building landlord's lien. The agricultural landlord's lien is covered in Sections 54.001 through 54.007 of the Property Code. The lien attaches essentially to the crops grown. Since most landlords who read this book are residential or commercial building landlords, the agricultural lien won't be discussed at length.

RESIDENTIAL LANDLORD'S LIEN

A residential landlord has a lien for all unpaid rent that is due on all non-exempt property of the tenant that is in the residence or stored in a storage room (§ 54.041).

EXEMPT
PROPERTY

The following items are considered to be exempt.

☞ Wearing apparel

☞ Tools, apparatus, and books of a trade or profession

☞ Schoolbooks

☞ A family library

☞ Family portraits and pictures

☞ One couch, two living room chairs, and a dining table and chairs

☞ Beds and bedding

☞ Kitchen furniture and utensils

☞ Food and food stuffs

☞ Medicine and medical supplies

☞ One automobile and one truck

☞ Agriculture implements

☞ Children's toys not commonly used by adults

☞ Goods that the landlord knows are owned by someone other than a tenant or occupant

☞ Goods the landlord knows are subject to a recorded chattel mortgage or financing agreement

Note: Things like TVs, stereos, and VCRs are not exempt.

SEIZURE OF
PROPERTY

A landlord's seizure of property is covered under § 54.044.

Abandoned Premises. The landlord may remove the contents of a leased premises the tenant has abandoned.

Other seizure. A landlord cannot seize exempt property. In order to seize non-exempt property, a written lease must authorize it, and it must be accomplished without a breach of the peace. In other words, you can't use force to seize and remove property while the tenant is there. If he's not present, you can use your key for entry and seize his non-exempt property.

Notice. Immediately after seizing the property, you must leave written notice of entry and an itemized list of the items removed in a conspicuous place in the dwelling. The notice must also state the amount of delinquent rent and the name, address, and telephone number of the person the tenant may contact regarding the rent.

The notice must also state that the property will be promptly returned on full payment of the back rent.

The landlord cannot collect a charge for packing, removing, or storing seized property unless specifically authorized in a written lease.

CONTRACTUAL LIEN

Some landlords like the added protection of a contractual lien where the tenant expressly grants a lien to the landlord. Such a lien is not valid unless it is underlined or printed in boldface type in the lease. However, no written agreement or contractual lien provision can waive or diminish the exemptions, rights, and liabilities under this statute. For example, an agreement to grant a contractual lien on a tenant's exempt property would be void and unforceable (§ 54.043).

SALE OF SEIZED PROPERTY

In order to sell any seized property, you must have a written lease that authorizes the sale. Otherwise, you would have to file suit to foreclose your lien. (Another good reason to have a written lease.) You must give the tenant notice not later than the thirtieth day before the date of the sale by both first class mail and certified mail, return receipt requested, at the tenant's last known address (§ 54.045). Your notice must include:

☞ The date, time and place of the sale

☞ An itemized account of the amount owed

☞ The name, address, and telephone number of the person the tenant can contact to pay up and redeem his property

Any sale to the highest bidder for cash and is subject to any chattel mortgage or financing statement. Sale proceeds must be applied first to delinquent rent and then to packing, removing, storage, and sale costs if authorized by the lease. These charges must be reasonable. If there is any money left over, you must send it to the tenant's last known address not less than thirty days after the sale. If the tenant makes a written request for an accounting, you must give him a written accounting within thirty days after his request.

REDEEMING THE
PROPERTY

The tenant may redeem his property any time before the sale by paying all money owed, including back rent, plus packing, moving, storage, and sale costs if authorized by the lease. If the landlord sues for unpaid rent, the tenant can recover (*replevy*) any property not sold by posting a bond in an amount approved by the court [§ 54.045(e)].

LANDLORD
VIOLATIONS

If the landlord violates this statute, the tenant can sue him, get actual damages, return of any unsold property, return of all proceeds of any sold property, plus a penalty of the greater of $500 or one month's rent, less any amount the tenant owes, plus attorney's fees (§ 54.046).

BUILDING LANDLORD'S LIEN

Under § 54.021, a building landlord has a preference lien on any tenant's property for rent due and to become due during the current twelve month period succeeding the date of the beginning of the rental agreement or an anniversary of that date. In other words, the lien only covers rent due for the current lease year. For example, if your five year lease on October 1, 1997 and today is January 19, 2000, you have a lien for any rent due from October 1, 1999 through September 30, 2000. If rent is due from before October 1, 1999, you don't have a lien for that rent. As a practical matter, what this means is that if there is $1,000 in back rent owed but $500 is from before October 1, 1999, and the tenant has $1,000 worth of property, you can only seize and sell $500 worth because that is all for which you have a lien. Therefore, you need to make sure you don't let past due rent accrue too long, or past the lease anniversary date, or your lien won't be valid for that back rent.

Also, the lien is unenforceable for rent on a commercial building that is more than six months past due unless the landlord file a lien statement with the county clerk. This lien statement must be verified by the landlord or his agent, and contain:

☞ The tenant's name and address

☞ A description (legal) of the leased premises

☞ The beginning and termination dates of the lease (§ 54.022)

☞ An account, itemized by month, of the past due rent for which the lien is claimed

The lien is not valid against any other property exempt under other law, such as a homestead exemption (§ 54.023).

The lien only exists while the tenant occupies the building and until one month after the day he abandons the building (§ 54.024).

ENFORCING A BUILDING LANDLORD'S LIEN

The statute does not provide a self-help seizure procedure as it does for a residential landlord. A building landlord can exercise his lien by one of two methods:

☞ File suit to foreclose the lien (hire an attorney).

☞ Apply to the justice of the peace for a distress warrant (§ 54.025). A distress warrant, if issued, orders the sheriff or constable to attach and hold the tenant's non-exempt property pending a final determination of the trial on rent. The landlord must show that the tenant:

• owes rent; and

• is about to abandon the building; or

• is about to remove the tenant's property from the building.

The procedure for distress warrant is contained in Rules 610 through 620, Texas Rules of Civil Procedure, and contain requirements for a bond, opportunity for the tenant to replevy or get it back by filing his own bond, and procedures for sale of perishable property.

Note: A landlord's lien is not necessary to obtain a distress warrant.

LAWSUIT FOR
RENT

Of course, if the tenant has moved out without leaving any property subject to your lien, you can still sue him to recover the past due rent. If the amount of rent due is less that $5,000, you can sue your former tenant in small claims court. If the amount of rent is over $5,000, you must sue in County Court at Law or District Court. If you can't use small claims court because the amount of rent you're suing for us too high, you are better off hiring an attorney. For more help on using small claims court, get a copy of *How to Win in Small Claims Court in Texas*, by William R. Brown and Mark Warda, available through your local bookstore, or directly from Sphinx Publishing by calling 1-800-226-5291.

MOBILE HOME PARKS AND SELF SERVICE STORAGE SPACE **12**

MOBILE HOME PARKS

A mobile home park landlord usually will have a contractual lien against the mobile home for unpaid rent for the mobile home lot or other real property where the mobile home is located (Texas Statutes, Article 5069-6A.18). This lien is subordinate (secondary) to a creditor with a security interest listed on the mobile home certificate of title.

However, if the landlord gives the creditor written notice by certified mail, return receipt requested, of unpaid rent and the creditor tries to repossess the mobile home, the landlord's lien has priority for any rent accrued after fifteen days after the notice is received, and any required grace period prior to repossession if the tenant has not voluntarily moved.

If the landlord has a valid lien, superior to the creditors, he or she can refuse to let the creditor move the mobile home. If the landlord does not have a superior lien, he or she can be liable to the creditor for damages, an injunction, attorney's fees, and court costs.

SELF SERVICE STORAGE FACILITIES

APPLICABLE
LAW

Chapter 59 of the Property Code gives the owner of a self-storage facility a priority lien against all property in the facility for the payment of charges due and unpaid by the tenant. It does not matter whose property it is, the lien attaches to any property in the unit on the date it is brought to the facility.

ENFORCEMENT

To enforce a self service storage facility lien, the landlord may only file suit to foreclose the lien; unless the written rental agreement provides, in underlined or bold print, a contractual landlord's lien with the right to seize and sell the property with filing suit. In such case, the landlord can seize and sell the property.

SEIZURE AND
SALE

If seizure and sale without a lawsuit is permitted by the written rental agreement, the following procedures must be followed.

Notice of Claim. The lessor must deliver a notice of claim in person or by certified mail, return receipt requested, to the tenant's last know address. The notice must include:

☞ The lessor's name, address, and telephone number

☞ An itemized account of the claim

☞ A statement that the contents of the self service storage facility have been seized under the contractual landlord's lien

☞ A statement that if the claim is not satisfied within fifteen days after mailing, the property may be sold at public auction

Notice of Sale. If fifteen days have passes without the claim being paid, the landlord must advertise the sale by either of the following methods:

☞ Publication of a notice of sale in each of two consecutive weeks in a newspaper of general circulation in the county where the facility is located

☞ If there is no such newspaper, by posting the notice of sale at the facility and in five other nearby conspicuous locations

The notice of sale must contain:

- ☛ A general description of the property
- ☛ A statement that the property is being sold to satisfy a landlord's liens
- ☛ The tenant's name
- ☛ The address of the facility
- ☛ The time, place, and terms of the sale

Conduct of Sale. The sale must be held no earlier than fifteen days after the first publication date or ten days after the posting date The sale must be by public auction, at or near the facility, according to the terms in the notice, and to the highest bidder. A good faith purchaser takes the property free of any claim against the property, even if the landlord did not follow the proper procedures.

If the proceeds of the sale are more than the amount of the lien and sales expenses, the landlord must send notice of the excess to the tenant's last known address. The landlord must keep the excess for two years and give it to the tenant if he requests it within the two years. After two years, the landlord owns. it.

A tenant may redeem seized property before sale by paying the landlord the amount of the lien and reasonable expenses.

APPENDIX A
EVICTION STATUTES AND RULES OF PROCEDURE

Because judges can be strict about court procedures, you need to carefully follow the rules when filing an eviction. One mistake may delay your case and cause you lost rent. This chapter contains the Texas statutes and rules of civil procedure which pertain to eviction proceedings, officially called Forcible Detainer. Be sure you understand and follow these rules when filing your case.

In addition to these laws, there are other Texas laws governing rental properties. Most of these are contained in Chapter 92 of the Property Code. You can find a copy of the Property Code in most public libraries and law libraries. The following portions of the law are included in this appendix:

- ☞ Property Code Chapter 24
- ☞ Property Code Chapter 91
- ☞ Property Code Chapter 92
- ☞ Civil Rules of Procedure, Rules 737 through 749

The following table will help you more quickly locate the particular chapter, section number, or rule you need.

CHAPTER 24. FORCIBLE ENTRY AND DETAINER

CHAPTER 91. PROVISIONS GENERALLY APPLICABLE TO LANDLORDS AND TENANTS

CHAPTER 92. RESIDENTIAL TENANCIES

SUBCHAPTER A. GENERAL PROVISIONS

SUBCHAPTER B. REPAIR OR CLOSING OF LEASEHOLD

SUBCHAPTER C. SECURITY DEPOSITS

SUBCHAPTER D. SECURITY DEVICES

CIVIL RULES OF PROCEDURE
Part VII. Rules Relating to Special Proceedings
Section 1. Bill of Discovery

Section 2. Forcible Entry and Detainer

Property Code
CHAPTER 24. FORCIBLE ENTRY AND DETAINER

Sec. 24.001. Forcible Entry and Detainer.

(a) A person commits a forcible entry and detainer if the person enters the real property of another without legal authority or by force and refuses to surrender possession on demand.

(b) For the purposes of this chapter, a forcible entry is:

(1) an entry without the consent of the person in actual possession of the property;

(2) an entry without the consent of a tenant at will or by sufferance; or

(3) an entry without the consent of a person who acquired possession by forcible entry.

Sec. 24.002. Forcible Detainer.

(a) A person who refuses to surrender possession of real property on demand commits a forcible detainer if the person:

(1) is a tenant or a subtenant wilfully and without force holding over after the termination of the tenant's right of possession;

(2) is a tenant at will or by sufferance, including an occupant at the time of foreclosure of a lien superior to the tenant's lease; or

(3) is a tenant of a person who acquired possession by forcible entry.

(b) The demand for possession must be made in writing by a person entitled to possession of the property and must comply with the requirements for notice to vacate under Section 24.005.

Sec. 24.003. Substitution of Parties.

If a tenancy for a term expires while the tenant's suit for forcible entry is pending, the landlord may prosecute the suit in the tenant's name for the landlord's benefit and at the landlord's expense. It is immaterial whether the tenant received possession from the landlord or became a tenant after obtaining possession of the property.

Sec. 24.004. Jurisdiction.

A justice court in the precinct in which the real property is located has jurisdiction in eviction suits. Eviction suits include forcible entry and detainer and forcible detainer suits.

Sec. 24.005. Notice to Vacate Prior to Filing Eviction Suit.

(a) If the occupant is a tenant under a written lease or oral rental agreement, the landlord must give a tenant who defaults or holds over beyond the end of the rental term or renewal period at least three days' written notice to vacate the premises before the landlord files a forcible detainer suit, unless the parties have contracted for a shorter or longer notice period in a written lease or agreement. A landlord who files a forcible detainer suit on grounds that the tenant is holding over beyond the end of the rental term or renewal period must also comply with the tenancy termination requirements of Section 91.001.

(b) If the occupant is a tenant at will or by sufferance, the landlord must give the tenant at least three days' written notice to vacate before the landlord files a forcible detainer suit unless the parties have contracted for a shorter or longer notice period in a written lease or agreement. If a building is purchased at a tax foreclosure sale or a trustee's foreclosure sale under a lien superior to the tenant's lease and the tenant timely pays rent and is not otherwise in default under the tenant's lease after foreclosure, the purchaser must give a residential tenant of the building at least 30 days' written notice to vacate if the purchaser chooses not to continue the lease. The tenant is considered to timely pay the rent under this subsection if, during the month of the foreclosure sale, the tenant pays the rent for that month to the landlord before receiving any notice that a foreclosure sale is scheduled during the month or pays the rent for that month to the foreclosing lienholder or the purchaser at foreclosure not later than the fifth day after the date of receipt of a written notice of the name and address of the purchaser that requests payment. Before a foreclosure sale, a foreclosing lienholder may give written notice to a tenant stating that a foreclosure notice has been given to the landlord or owner of the property and specifying the date of the foreclosure.

(c) If the occupant is a tenant of a person who acquired possession by forcible entry, the landlord must give the person at least three days' written notice to vacate before the landlord files a forcible detainer suit.

(d) In all situations in which the entry by the occupant was a forcible entry under Section 24.001, the person entitled to possession must give the occupant oral or written notice to vacate before the landlord files a forcible entry and detainer suit. The notice to vacate under this subsection may be to vacate immediately or by a specified deadline.

(e) If the lease or applicable law requires the landlord to give a tenant an opportunity to respond to a notice of proposed eviction, a notice to vacate may not be given until the period provided for the tenant to respond to the eviction notice has expired.

(f) The notice to vacate shall be given in person or by mail at the premises in question. Notice in person may be by personal delivery to the tenant or any person residing at the premises who is 16 years of age or older or personal delivery to the premises and affixing the notice to the inside of the main entry door. Notice by mail may be by regular mail, by registered mail, or by certified mail, return receipt requested, to the premises in question. If the dwelling has no mailbox and has a keyless bolting device, alarm system, or dangerous animal that prevents the landlord from entering the premises to leave the notice to vacate on the inside of the main entry door, the landlord may securely affix the notice on the outside of the main entry door.

(g) The notice period is calculated from the day on which the notice is delivered.

(h) A notice to vacate shall be considered a demand for possession for purposes of Subsection (b) of Section 24.002.

(i) If before the notice to vacate is given as required by this section the landlord has given a written notice or reminder to the tenant that rent is due and unpaid, the landlord may include in the notice to vacate required by this section a demand that the tenant pay the delinquent rent or vacate the premises by the date and time stated in the notice.

Sec. 24.006. Attorney's Fees and Costs of Suit.

(a) Except as provided by Subsection (b), to be eligible to recover attorney's fees in an eviction suit, a landlord must give a tenant who is unlawfully retaining possession of the landlord's premises a written demand to vacate the premises. The demand must state that if the tenant does not vacate the premises before the 11th day after the date of receipt of the notice and if the landlord files suit, the landlord may recover attorney's fees.

The demand must be sent by registered mail or by certified mail, return receipt requested, at least 10 days before the date the suit is filed.

(b) If the landlord provides the tenant notice under Subsection (a) or if a written lease entitles the landlord to recover attorney's fees, a prevailing landlord is entitled to recover reasonable attorney's fees from the tenant.

(c) If the landlord provides the tenant notice under Subsection (a) or if a written lease entitles the landlord or the tenant to recover attorney's fees, the prevailing tenant is entitled to recover reasonable attorney's fees from the landlord. A prevailing tenant is not required to give notice in order to recover attorney's fees under this subsection.

(d) The prevailing party is entitled to recover all costs of court.

Sec. 24.0061. Writ of Possession.

(a) A landlord who prevails in an eviction suit is entitled to a judgment for possession of the premises and a writ of possession. In this chapter, "premises" means the unit that is occupied or rented and any outside area or facility that the tenant is entitled to use under a written lease or oral rental agreement, or that is held out for the use of tenants generally.

(b) A writ of possession may not be issued before the sixth day after the date on which the judgment for possession is rendered unless a possession bond has been filed and approved under the Texas Rules of Civil Procedure and judgment for possession is thereafter granted by default.

(c) The court shall notify a tenant in writing of a default judgment for possession by sending a copy of the judgment to the premises by first class mail not later than 48 hours after the entry of the judgment.

(d) The writ of possession shall order the officer executing the writ to:

(1) post a written warning of at least 8 1/2 by 11 inches on the exterior of the front door of the rental unit notifying the tenant that the writ has been issued and that the writ will be executed on or after a specific date and time stated in the warning not sooner than 24 hours after the warning is posted; and

(2) when the writ is executed:

(A) deliver possession of the premises to the landlord;

(B) instruct the tenant and all persons claiming under the tenant to leave the premises immediately, and, if the persons fail to comply, physically remove them;

(C) instruct the tenant to remove or to allow the landlord, the landlord's representatives, or other persons acting under the officer's supervision to remove all personal property from the rental unit other than personal property claimed to be owned by the landlord; and

(D) place, or have an authorized person place, the removed personal property outside the rental unit at a nearby location, but not blocking a public sidewalk, passageway, or street and not while it is raining, sleeting, or snowing.

(e) The writ of possession shall authorize the officer, at the officer's discretion, to engage the services of a bonded or insured warehouseman to remove and store, subject to applicable law, part or all of the property at no cost to the landlord or the officer executing the writ.

(f) The officer may not require the landlord to store the property.

(g) The writ of possession shall contain notice to the officer that under Section 7.003, Civil Practice and Remedies Code, the officer is not liable for damages resulting from the execution of the writ if the officer executes the writ in good faith and with reasonable diligence.

(h) A sheriff or constable may use reasonable force in executing a writ under this section.

Sec. 24.0062. Warehouseman's Lien.

(a) If personal property is removed from a tenant's premises as the result of an action brought under this chapter and stored in a bonded or insured public warehouse, the warehouseman has a lien on the property to the extent of any reasonable storage and moving charges incurred by the warehouseman. The lien does not attach to any property until the property has been stored by the warehouseman.

(b) If property is to be removed and stored in a public warehouse under a writ of possession, the officer executing the writ shall, at the time of execution, deliver in person to the tenant, or by first class mail to the tenant's last known address not later than 72 hours after execution of the writ if the tenant is not present, a written notice stating the complete address and telephone number of the location at which the property may be redeemed and stating that:

(1) the tenant's property is to be removed and stored by a public warehouseman under Section 24.0062 of the Property Code;

(2) the tenant may redeem any of the property, without payment of moving or storage charges, on demand during the time the warehouseman is removing the property from the tenant's premises and before the warehouseman permanently leaves the tenant's premises;

(3) within 30 days from the date of storage, the tenant may redeem any of the property described by Section 24.0062(e), Property Code, on demand by the tenant and on payment of the moving and storage charges reasonably attributable to the items being redeemed;

(4) after the 30-day period and before sale, the tenant may redeem the property on demand by the tenant and on payment of all moving and storage charges; and

(5) subject to the previously stated conditions, the warehouseman has a lien on the property to secure payment of moving and storage charges and may sell all the property to satisfy reasonable moving and storage charges after 30 days, subject to the requirements of Section 24.0062(j) of the Property Code.

(c) The statement required by Subsection (b)(2) must be underlined or in boldfaced print.

(d) On demand by the tenant during the time the warehouseman is removing the property from the tenant's premises and before the warehouseman permanently leaves the tenant's premises, the warehouseman shall return to the tenant all property requested by the tenant, without charge.

(e) On demand by the tenant within 30 days after the date the property is stored by the warehouseman and on payment by the tenant of the moving and storage charges reasonably attributable to the items being redeemed, the warehouseman shall return to the tenant at the warehouse the following property:

(1) wearing apparel;

(2) tools, apparatus, and books of a trade or profession;

(3) school books;

(4) a family library;

(5) family portraits and pictures;

(6) one couch, two living room chairs, and a dining table and chairs;

(7) beds and bedding;

(8) kitchen furniture and utensils;

(9) food and foodstuffs;

(10) medicine and medical supplies;

(11) one automobile and one truck;

(12) agricultural implements;

(13) children's toys not commonly used by adults;

(14) goods that the warehouseman or the warehouseman's agent knows are owned by a person other than the tenant or an occupant of the residence;

(15) goods that the warehouseman or the warehouseman's agent knows are subject to a recorded chattel mortgage or financing agreement; and

(16) cash.

(f) During the first 30 days after the date of storage, the warehouseman may not require payment of removal or storage charges for other items as a condition for redeeming the items described by Subsection (e).

(g) On demand by the tenant to the warehouseman after the 30-day period and before sale and on payment by the tenant of all unpaid moving and storage charges on all the property, the warehouseman shall return all the previously unredeemed property to the tenant at the warehouse.

(h) A warehouseman may not recover any moving or storage charges if the court determines under Subsection (i) that the warehouseman's moving or storage charges are not reasonable.

(i) Before the sale of the property by the warehouseman, the tenant may file suit in the justice court in which the eviction judgment was rendered, or in another court of competent jurisdiction in the county in which the rental premises are located, to recover the property described by Subsection (e) on the ground that the landlord failed to return the property after timely demand and payment by the tenant, as provided by this section. Before sale, the tenant may also file suit to recover all property moved or stored by the warehouseman on the ground that the amount of the warehouseman's moving or storage charges is not reasonable. All proceedings under this subsection have precedence over other matters on the court's docket. The justice court that issued the writ of possession has jurisdiction under this section regardless of the amount in controversy.

(j) Any sale of property that is subject to a lien under this section shall be conducted in accordance with Sections 7.210, 9.301-9.318, and .0 9.501-9.507 of the Business & Commerce Code.

(k) In a proceeding under this section, the prevailing party is entitled to recover actual damages, reasonable attorney's fees, court costs, and, if appropriate, any property withheld in violation of this section or the value of that property if it has been sold.

Appeal.

A final judgment of a county court in an eviction suit may not be appealed on the issue of possession unless the premises in question are being used for residential purposes only. A judgment of a county court may not under any circumstances be stayed pending appeal unless, within 10 days of the signing of the judgment, the appellant files a supersedeas bond in an amount set by the county court. In setting the supersedeas bond the county court shall provide protection for the appellee to the same extent as in any other appeal, taking into consideration the value of rents likely to accrue during appeal, damages which may occur as a result of the stay during appeal, and other damages or amounts as the court may deem appropriate.

Sec. 24.008. Effect on Other Actions.

An eviction suit does not bar a suit for trespass, damages, waste, rent, or mesne profits.

Sec. 24.011. Nonlawyer Representation.

In eviction suits in justice court for nonpayment of rent or holding over beyond a rental term, the parties may represent themselves or be represented by their authorized agents, who need not be attorneys. In any eviction suit in justice court, an authorized agent requesting or obtaining a default judgment need not be an attorney.

Property Code
CHAPTER 91. PROVISIONS GENERALLY APPLICABLE TO LANDLORDS AND TENANTS

Sec. 91.001. Notice for Terminating Certain Tenancies.

(a) A monthly tenancy or a tenancy from month to month may be terminated by the tenant or the landlord giving notice of termination to the other.

(b) If a notice of termination is given under Subsection (a) and if the rent-paying period is at least one month, the tenancy terminates on whichever of the following days is the later:

(1) the day given in the notice for termination; or

(2) one month after the day on which the notice is given.

(c) If a notice of termination is given under Subsection (a) and if the rent-paying period is less than a month, the tenancy terminates on whichever of the following days is the later:

(1) the day given in the notice for termination; or

(2) the day following the expiration of the period beginning on the day on which notice is given and extending for a number of days equal to the number of days in the rent-paying period.

(d) If a tenancy terminates on a day that does not correspond to the beginning or end of a rent-playing period, the tenant is liable for rent only up to the date of termination.

(e) Subsections (a), (b), (c), and (d) do not apply if:

(1) a landlord and a tenant have agreed in an instrument signed by both parties on a different period of notice to terminate the tenancy or that no notice is required; or

(2) there is a breach of contract recognized by law.

Sec. 91.003. Termination of Lease Because of Public Indecency Conviction.

(a) A landlord may terminate a lease executed or renewed after June 15, 1981, if:

(1) the tenant or occupant of the leasehold uses the property for an activity for which the tenant or occupant or for which an agent or employee of the tenant or occupant is convicted under Chapter 43, Penal Code, as amended; and

(2) the convicted person has exhausted or abandoned all avenues or direct appeal from the conviction.

(b) The fee owner or an intermediate lessor terminates the lease by giving written notice of termination to the tenant or occupant within six months after the right to terminate arises under this section. The right to possess the property reverts to the landlord on the 10th day after the date the notice is given.

(c) This section applies regardless of a term of the lease to the contrary.

Sec. 91.004. Landlord's Breach of Lease; Lien.

(a) If the landlord of a tenant who is not in default under a lease fails to comply in any respect with the lease agreement, the landlord is liable to the tenant for damages resulting from the failure.

(b) To secure payment of the damages, the tenant has a lien on the landlord's nonexempt property in the tenant's possession and on the rent due to the landlord under the lease.

Sec. 91.005. Subletting Prohibited.

During the term of a lease, the tenant may not rent the leasehold to any other person without the prior consent of the landlord.

Sec. 91.006. Landlord's Duty to Mitigate Damages.

(a) A landlord has a duty to mitigate damages if a tenant abandons the leased premises in violation of the lease.

(b) A provision of a lease that purports to waive a right or to exempt a landlord from a liability or duty under this section is void.

Property Code
CHAPTER 92. RESIDENTIAL TENANCIES

SUBCHAPTER A. GENERAL PROVISIONS

Sec. 92.001. Definitions.

Except as otherwise provided by this chapter, in this chapter:

(1) "Dwelling" means one or more rooms rented for use as a permanent residence under a single lease to one or more tenants.

(2) "Landlord" means the owner, lessor, or sublessor of a dwelling, but does not include a manager or agent of the landlord unless the manager or agent purports to be the owner, lessor, or sublessor in an oral or written lease.

(3) "Lease" means any written or oral agreement between a landlord and tenant that establishes or modifies the terms, conditions, rules, or other provisions regarding the use and occupancy of a dwelling.

(4) "Normal wear and tear" means deterioration that results from the intended use of a dwelling, including, for the purposes of Subchapters B and D, breakage or malfunction due to age or deteriorated condition, but the term does not include deterioration that results from negligence, carelessness, accident, or abuse of the premises, equipment, or chattels by the tenant, by a member of the tenant's household, or by a guest or invitee of the tenant.

(5) "Premises" means a tenant's rental unit, any area or facility the lease authorizes the tenant to use, and the appurtenances, grounds, and facilities held out for the use of tenants generally.

(6) "Tenant" means a person who is authorized by a lease to occupy a dwelling to the exclusion of others and, for the purposes of Subchapters D, E, and F, who is obligated under the lease to pay rent.

Sec. 92.002. Application.

This chapter applies only to the relationship between landlords and tenants of residential rental property.

Sec. 92.003. Landlord's Agent for Service of Process.

(a) In a lawsuit by a tenant under either a written or oral lease for a dwelling or in a suit to enforce a legal obligation of the owner as landlord of the dwelling, the owner's agent for service of process is determined according to this section.

(b) If written notice of the name and business street address of the company that manages the dwelling has been given to the
tenant, the management company is the owner's sole agent for service of process.

(c) If Subsection (b) does not apply, the owner's management company, on-premise manager, or rent collector serving the dwelling is the owner's authorized agent for service of process unless the owner's name and business street address have been furnished in writing to the tenant.

Sec. 92.004. Harassment.

A party who files or prosecutes a suit under Subchapter B, D, E, or F in bad faith or for purposes of harassment is liable to the defendant for one month's rent plus $100 and for attorney's fees.

Sec. 92.005. Attorney's Fees.

(a) A party who prevails in a suit brought under Subchapter B, E, or F may recover the party's costs of court and reasonable attorney's fees in relation to work reasonably expended.

(b) This section does not authorize a recovery of attorney's fees in an action brought under Subchapter E or F for damages that relate to or arise from property damage, personal injury, or a criminal act.

Sec. 92.006. Waiver or Expansion of Duties and Remedies.

(a) A landlord's duty or a tenant's remedy concerning security deposits, security devices, the landlord's disclosure of ownership and management, or utility cutoffs, as provided by Subchapter C, D, E, or G, respectively, may not be waived. A landlord's duty to install a smoke detector under Subchapter F may not be waived, nor may a tenant waive a remedy for the landlord's noninstallation or waive the tenant's limited right of installation and removal. The landlord's duty of inspection and repair of smoke detectors under Subchapter F may be waived only by written agreement.

(b) A landlord's duties and the tenant's remedies concerning security devices, the landlord's disclosure of ownership and management, or smoke detectors, as provided by Subchapter D, E, or F, respectively, may be enlarged only by specific written agreement.

(c) A landlord's duties and the tenant's remedies under Subchapter B, which covers conditions materially affecting the physical health or safety of the ordinary tenant, may not be waived except as provided in Subsections (d), (e), and (f) of this section.

(d) A landlord and a tenant may agree for the tenant to repair or remedy, at the landlord's expense, any condition covered by Subchapter B.

(e) A landlord and a tenant may agree for the tenant to repair or remedy, at the tenant's expense, any condition covered by Subchapter B if all of the following conditions are met:

(1) at the beginning of the lease term the landlord owns only one rental dwelling;

(2) at the beginning of the lease term the dwelling is free from any condition which would materially affect the physical health or safety of an ordinary tenant;

(3) at the beginning of the lease term the landlord has no reason to believe that any condition described in Subdivision (2) of this subsection is likely to occur or recur during the tenant's lease term or during a renewal or extension; and

(4) (A) the lease is in writing;

(B) the agreement for repairs by the tenant is either underlined or printed in boldface in the lease or in a separate written addendum;

(C) the agreement is specific and clear; and

(D) the agreement is made knowingly, voluntarily, and for consideration.

(f) A landlord and tenant may agree that, except for those conditions caused by the negligence of the landlord, the tenant has the duty to pay for repair of the following conditions that may occur during the lease term or a renewal or extension:

(1) damage from wastewater stoppages caused by foreign or improper objects in lines that exclusively serve the tenant's dwelling;

(2) damage to doors, windows, or screens; and

(3) damage from windows or doors left open.

This subsection shall not affect the landlord's duty under Subchapter B to repair or remedy, at the landlord's expense, wastewater stoppages or backups caused by deterioration, breakage, roots, ground conditions, faulty construction, or malfunctioning equipment. A landlord and tenant may agree to the

provisions of this subsection only if the agreement meets the requirements of Subdivision (4) of Subsection (e) of this section.

Sec. 92.007. Venue.

Venue for an action under this chapter is governed by Section 15.0115, Civil Practice and Remedies Code.

Sec. 92.008. Interruption of Utilities.

(a) A landlord or a landlord's agent may not interrupt or cause the interruption of utility service paid for directly to the utility company by a tenant unless the interruption results from bona fide repairs, construction, or an emergency.

(b) Except as provided by Subsections (c) and (d), a landlord may not interrupt or cause the interruption of water, wastewater, gas, or electric service furnished to a tenant by the landlord as an incident of the tenancy or by other agreement unless the interruption results from bona fide repairs, construction, or an emergency.

(c) A landlord may interrupt or cause the interruption of electrical service furnished to a tenant by the landlord as an incident of the tenancy or by other agreement if:

(1) the electrical service furnished to the tenant is individually metered or submetered for the dwelling unit;

(2) the electrical service connection with the utility company is in the name of the landlord or the landlord's agent; and

(3) the landlord complies with the rules adopted by the Public Utility Commission of Texas for discontinuance of submetered electrical service.

(d) A landlord may interrupt or cause the interruption of electrical service furnished to a tenant by the landlord as an incident of the tenancy or by other agreement if:

(1) the electrical service furnished to the tenant is not individually metered or submetered for the dwelling unit;

(2) the electrical service connection with the utility company is in the name of the landlord or the landlord's agent;

(3) the tenant is at least seven days late in paying the rent;

(4) the landlord has mailed or hand-delivered to the tenant at least five days before the date

the electrical service is interrupted a written notice that states:

(A) the earliest date of the proposed interruption of electrical service;

(B) the amount of rent the tenant must pay to avert the interruption; and

(C) the name and location of the individual to whom or the location of the on-site management office where the delinquent rent may be paid during the landlord's normal business hours;

(5) the interruption does not begin before or after the landlord's normal business hours; and

(6) the interruption does not begin on a day, or on a day immediately preceding a day, when the landlord or other designated individual is not available or the on-site management office is not open to accept rent and restore electrical service.

(e) A landlord who interrupts electrical service under Subsection (c) or (d) shall restore the service not later than two hours after the time the tenant tenders, during the landlord's normal business hours, payment of the delinquent electric bill or rent owed to the landlord.

(f) If a landlord or a landlord's agent violates this section, the tenant may:

(1) either recover possession of the premises or terminate the lease; and

(2) recover from the landlord an amount equal to the sum of the tenant's actual damages, one month's rent or $500, whichever is greater, reasonable attorney's fees, and court costs, less any delinquent rents or other sums for which the tenant is liable to the landlord.

(g) A provision of a lease that purports to waive a right or to exempt a party from a liability or duty under this section is void.

Sec. 92.0081. Removal of Property and Exclusion of Residential Tenant.

(a) A landlord may not remove a door, window, or attic hatchway cover or a lock, latch, hinge, hinge pin, doorknob, or other mechanism connected to a door, window, or attic hatchway cover from premises leased to a tenant or remove furniture, fixtures, or appliances furnished by the landlord from premises leased to a tenant unless the landlord removes the item for a bona fide repair or replacement. If a landlord removes any of the items listed in this

subsection for a bona fide repair or replacement, the repair or replacement must be promptly performed.

(b) A landlord may not intentionally prevent a tenant from entering the leased premises except by judicial process unless the exclusion results from:

(1) bona fide repairs, construction, or an emergency;

(2) removing the contents of premises abandoned by a tenant; or

(3) changing the door locks of a tenant who is delinquent in paying at least part of the rent.

(c) If a landlord or a landlord's agent changes the door lock of a tenant who is delinquent in paying rent, the landlord or the landlord's agent must place a written notice on the tenant's front door stating:

(1) an on-site location where the tenant may go 24 hours a day to obtain the new key or a telephone number that is answered 24 hours a day that the tenant may call to have a key delivered within two hours after calling the number;

(2) the fact that the landlord must provide the new key to the tenant at any hour, regardless of whether or not the tenant pays any of the delinquent rent; and

(3) the amount of rent and other charges for which the tenant is delinquent.

(d) A landlord may not intentionally prevent a tenant from entering the leased premises under Subsection (b)(3) unless:

(1) the tenant is delinquent in paying all or part of the rent; and

(2) the landlord has locally mailed not later than the fifth calendar day before the date on which the door locks are changed or hand-delivered to the tenant or posted on the inside of the main entry door of the tenant's dwelling not later than the third calendar day before the date on which the door locks are changed a written notice stating:

(A) the earliest date that the landlord proposes to change the door locks;

(B) the amount of rent the tenant must pay to prevent changing of the door locks; and

(C) the name and street address of the individual to whom, or the location of the on-site management office at which, the delinquent rent may be paid during the landlord's normal business hours.

(e) A landlord may not change the locks on the door of a tenant's dwelling under Subsection (b)(3) on a day, or on a day immediately before a day, on which the landlord or other designated individual is not available, or on which any on-site management office is not open, for the tenant to tender the delinquent rent.

(f) A landlord who intentionally prevents a tenant from entering the tenant's dwelling under Subsection (b)(3) must provide the tenant with a key to the changed lock on the dwelling without regard to whether the tenant pays the delinquent rent.

(g) If a landlord arrives at the dwelling in a timely manner in response to a tenant's telephone call to the number contained in the notice as described by Subsection (c)(1) and the tenant is not present to receive the key to the changed lock, the landlord shall leave a notice on the front door of the dwelling stating the time the landlord arrived with the key and the street address to which the tenant may go to obtain the key during the landlord's normal office hours.

(h) If a landlord violates this section, the tenant may:

(1) either recover possession of the premises or terminate the lease; and

(2) recover from the landlord a civil penalty of one month's rent plus $500, actual damages, court costs, and reasonable attorney's fees in an action to recover property damages, actual expenses, or civil penalties , less any delinquent rent or other sums for which the tenant is liable to the landlord.

(i) If a landlord violates Subsection (f), the tenant may recover, in addition to the remedies provided by Subsection (h), an additional civil penalty of one month's rent.

(j) A provision of a lease that purports to waive a right or to exempt a party from a liability or duty under this section is void.

Sec. 92.009. Residential Tenant's Right of Reentry After Unlawful Lockout.

(a) If a landlord has locked a tenant out of leased premises in violation of Section 92.008, the tenant may recover possession of the premises as provided by this section.

(b) The tenant must file with the justice court in the precinct in which the rental premises are located a sworn complaint for reentry, specifying the facts of the alleged unlawful lockout by the landlord or the landlord's agent. The tenant must also state orally under oath to the justice the facts of the alleged unlawful lockout.

(c) If the tenant has complied with Subsection (b) and if the justice reasonably believes an unlawful lockout has likely occurred, the justice may issue, ex parte, a writ of reentry that entitles the tenant to immediate and temporary possession of the premises, pending a final hearing on the tenant's sworn complaint for reentry.

(d) The writ of reentry must be served on either the landlord or the landlord's management company, on-premises manager, or rent collector in the same manner as a writ of possession in a forcible detainer action. A sheriff or constable may use reasonable force in executing a writ of reentry under this section.

(e) The landlord is entitled to a hearing on the tenant's sworn complaint for reentry. The writ of reentry must notify the landlord of the right to a hearing. The hearing shall be held not earlier than the first day and not later than the seventh day after the date the landlord requests a hearing.

(f) If the landlord fails to request a hearing on the tenant's sworn complaint for reentry before the eighth day after the date of service of the writ of reentry on the landlord under Subsection (d), a judgment for court costs may be rendered against the landlord.

(g) A party may appeal from the court's judgment at the hearing on the sworn complaint for reentry in the same manner as a party may appeal a judgment in a forcible detainer suit.

(h) If a writ of possession is issued, it supersedes a writ of reentry.

(i) If the landlord or the person on whom a writ of reentry is served fails to immediately comply with the writ or later disobeys the writ, the failure is grounds for contempt of court against the landlord or the person on whom the writ was served, under Section 21.002, Government Code. If the writ is disobeyed, the tenant or the tenant's attorney may file in the court in which the reentry action is pending an affidavit stating the name of the person who has disobeyed the writ and describing the acts or omissions constituting the disobedience. On receipt of an affidavit, the justice shall issue a show cause order, directing the person to appear on a designated date and show cause why he should not be adjudged in contempt of court. If the justice finds, after considering the evidence at the hearing, that the person has directly or indirectly disobeyed the writ, the justice may commit the person to jail without bail until the person purges himself of the contempt in a manner and form as the justice may direct. If the person disobeyed the writ before receiving the show cause order but has complied with the writ after receiving the order, the justice may find the person in contempt and assess punishment under Section 21.002(c), Government Code.

(j) This section does not affect a tenant's right to pursue a separate cause of action under Section 92.008.

(k) If a tenant in bad faith files a sworn complaint for reentry resulting in a writ of reentry being served on the landlord or landlord's agent, the landlord may in a separate cause of action recover from the tenant an amount equal to actual damages, one month's rent or $500, whichever is greater, reasonable attorney's fees, and costs of court, less any sums for which the landlord is liable to the tenant.

(l) The fee for filing a sworn complaint for reentry is the same as that for filing a civil action in justice court. The fee for service of a writ of reentry is the same as that for service of a writ of possession. The fee for service of a show cause order is the same as that for service of a civil citation. The justice may defer payment of the tenant's filing fees and service costs for the sworn complaint for reentry and writ of reentry. Court costs may be waived only if the tenant executes a pauper's affidavit.

(m) This section does not affect the rights of a landlord or tenant in a forcible detainer or forcible entry and detainer action.

Sec. 92.010. Occupancy Limits.

(a) Except as provided by Subsection (b), the maximum number of adults that a landlord may allow to occupy a dwelling is three times the number of bedrooms in the dwelling.

(b) A landlord may allow an occupancy rate of more than three adult tenants per bedroom:

(1) to the extent that the landlord is required by a state or federal fair housing law to allow a higher occupancy rate; or

(2) if an adult whose occupancy causes a violation of Subsection (a) is seeking temporary sanctuary from family violence, as

defined by Section 71.01, Family Code, for a period that does not exceed one month.

(c) An individual who owns or leases a dwelling within 3,000 feet of a dwelling as to which a landlord has violated this section, or a governmental entity or civic association acting on behalf of the individual, may file suit against a landlord to enjoin the violation. A party who prevails in a suit under this subsection may recover court costs and reasonable attorney's fees from the other party. In addition to court costs and reasonable attorney's fees, a plaintiff who prevails under this subsection may recover from the landlord $500 for each violation of this section.

(d) In this section:

(1) "Adult" means an individual 18 years of age or older.

(2) "Bedroom" means an area of a dwelling intended as sleeping quarters. The term does not include a kitchen, dining room, bathroom, living room, utility room, or closet or storage area of a dwelling.

Sec. 92.011. Cash Rental Payments.

(a) A landlord shall accept a tenant's timely cash rental payment unless a written lease between the landlord and tenant requires the tenant to make rental payments by check, money order, or other traceable or negotiable instrument.

(b) A landlord who receives a cash rental payment shall:

(1) provide the tenant with a written receipt; and

(2) enter the payment date and amount in a record book maintained by the landlord.

(c) A tenant or a governmental entity or civic association acting on the tenant's behalf may file suit against a landlord to enjoin a violation of this section. A party who prevails in a suit brought under this subsection may recover court costs and reasonable attorney's fees from the other party. In addition to court costs and reasonable attorney's fees, a tenant who prevails under this subsection may recover from the landlord the greater of one month's rent or $500 for each violation of this section.

Sec. 92.012. Notice to Tenant at Primary Residence.

(a) If, at the time of signing a lease or lease renewal, a tenant gives written notice to the tenant's landlord that the tenant does not occupy the leased premises as a primary residence and requests in writing that the landlord send notices to the tenant at the tenant's primary residence and provides to the landlord the address of the tenant's primary residence, the landlord shall mail to the tenant's primary residence:

(1) all notices of lease violations;

(2) all notices of lease termination;

(3) all notices of rental increases at the end of the lease term; and

(4) all notices to vacate.

(b) The tenant shall notify the landlord in writing of any change in the tenant's primary residence address. Oral notices of change are insufficient.

(c) A notice to a tenant's primary residence under Subsection (a) may be sent by regular United States mail and shall be considered as having been given on the date of postmark of the notice.

(d) If there is more than one tenant on a lease, the landlord is not required under this section to send notices to the primary residence of more than one tenant.

(e) This section does not apply if notice is actually hand delivered to and received by a person occupying the leased premises.

SUBCHAPTER B. REPAIR OR
CLOSING OF LEASEHOLD

Sec. 92.051. Application.

This subchapter applies to a lease executed, entered into, renewed, or extended on or after September 1, 1979.

Sec. 92.052. Landlord's Duty to Repair or Remedy.

(a) A landlord shall make a diligent effort to repair or remedy a condition if:

(1) the tenant specifies the condition in a notice to the person to whom or to the place where rent is normally paid;

(2) the tenant is not delinquent in the payment of rent at the time notice is given; and

(3) the condition materially affects the physical health or safety of an ordinary tenant.

(b) Unless the condition was caused by normal wear and tear, the landlord does not have a duty during the lease term or a renewal or extension to repair or remedy a condition caused by:

(1) the tenant;

(2) a lawful occupant in the tenant's dwelling;

(3) a member of the tenant's family; or

(4) a guest or invitee of the tenant.

(c) This subchapter does not require the landlord:

(1) to furnish utilities from a utility company if as a practical matter the utility lines of the company are not reasonably available; or

(2) to furnish security guards.

(d) The tenant's notice under Subsection (a) must be in writing only if the tenant's lease is in writing and requires written notice.

Sec. 92.053. Burden of Proof.

(a) Except as provided by this section, the tenant has the burden of proof in a judicial action to enforce a right resulting from the landlord's failure to repair or remedy a condition under Section 92.052.

(b) If the landlord does not provide a written explanation for delay in performing a duty to repair or remedy on or before the fifth day after receiving from the tenant a written demand for an explanation, the landlord has the burden of proving that he made a diligent effort to repair and that a reasonable time for repair did not elapse.

Sec. 92.054. Casualty Loss.

(a) If a condition results from an insured casualty loss, such as fire, smoke, hail, explosion, or a similar cause, the period for repair does not begin until the landlord receives the insurance proceeds.

(b) If after a casualty loss the rental premises are as a practical matter totally unusable for residential purposes and if the casualty loss is not caused by the negligence or fault of the tenant, a member of the tenant's family, or a guest or invitee of the tenant, either the landlord or the tenant may terminate the lease by giving written notice to the other any time before repairs are completed. If the lease is terminated, the tenant is entitled only to a pro rata refund of rent from the date the tenant moves out and to a refund of any security deposit otherwise required by law.

(c) If after a casualty loss the rental premises are partially unusable for residential purposes and if the casualty loss is not caused by the negligence or fault of the tenant, a member of the tenant's family, or a guest or invitee of the tenant, the tenant is entitled to reduction in the rent in an amount proportionate to the extent the premises are unusable because of the casualty, but only on judgment of a county or district court. A landlord and tenant may agree otherwise in a written lease.

Sec. 92.055. Closing the Rental Premises.

(a) A landlord may close a rental unit at any time by giving written notice by certified mail, return receipt requested, to the tenant and to the local health officer and local building inspector, if any, stating that:

(1) the landlord is terminating the tenancy as soon as legally possible; and

(2) after the tenant moves out the landlord will either immediately demolish the rental unit or no longer use the unit for residential purposes.

(b) After a tenant receives the notice and moves out:

(1) the local health officer or building inspector may not allow occupancy of or utility service by separate meter to the rental unit until the officer certifies that he knows of no condition that materially affects the physical health or safety of an ordinary tenant; and

(2) the landlord may not allow reoccupancy or reconnection of utilities by separate meter within six months after the date the tenant moves out.

(c) If the landlord gives the tenant the notice closing the rental unit:

(1) before the tenant gives a repair notice to the landlord, the remedies of this subchapter do not apply;

(2) after the tenant gives a repair notice to the landlord but before the landlord has had a reasonable time to make repairs, the tenant is entitled only to the remedies under Subsection (d) of this section and Subdivisions (3), (4), and (5) of Subsection (a) of Section 92.0563; or

(3) after the tenant gives a repair notice to the landlord and after the landlord has had a reasonable time to make repairs, the tenant is entitled only to the remedies under Subsection (d) of this section and Subdivisions (3), (4), and (5) of Subsection (a) of Section 92.0563.

(d) If the landlord closes the rental unit after the tenant gives the landlord a notice to repair and the tenant moves out on or before the end of the rental term, the landlord must pay the tenant's actual and reasonable moving expenses, refund a pro rata portion of the tenant's rent from the date the tenant moves out, and, if otherwise required by law, return the tenant's security deposit.

(e) A landlord who violates Subsection (b) or (d) is liable to the tenant for an amount equal to the total of one month's rent plus $100 and attorney's fees.

(f) The closing of a rental unit does not prohibit the occupancy of other apartments, nor does this subchapter prohibit occupancy of or utility service by master or individual meter to other rental units in an apartment complex that have not been closed under this section. If another provision of this subchapter conflicts with this section, this section controls.

Sec. 92.056. Landlord Liability and Tenant Remedies; Notice and Time for Repair.

(a) A landlord's liability under this section is subject to Section 92.052(b) regarding conditions that are caused by a tenant and Section 92.054 regarding conditions that are insured casualties.

(b) A landlord is liable to a tenant as provided by this subchapter if:

(1) the tenant has given the landlord notice to repair or remedy a condition by giving that notice to the person to whom or to the place where the tenant's rent is normally paid;

(2) the condition materially affects the physical health or safety of an ordinary tenant;

(3) the tenant has given the landlord a subsequent written notice to repair or remedy the condition after a reasonable time to repair or remedy the condition following the notice given under Subdivision (1) or the tenant has given the notice under Subdivision (1) by sending that notice by certified mail, return receipt requested, or by registered mail;

(4) the landlord has had a reasonable time to repair or remedy the condition after the landlord received the tenant's notice under Subdivision (1) and, if applicable, the tenant's subsequent notice under Subdivision (3);

(5) the landlord has not made a diligent effort to repair or remedy the condition after the landlord received the tenant's notice under Subdivision (1) and, if applicable, the tenant's notice under Subdivision (3); and

(6) the tenant was not delinquent in the payment of rent at the time any notice required by this subsection was given.

(c) For purposes of Subsection (b)(4) or (5), a landlord is considered to have received the tenant's notice when the landlord or the landlord's agent or employee has actually received the notice or when the United States Postal Service has attempted to deliver the notice to the landlord.

(d) For purposes of Subsection (b)(3) or (4), in determining whether a period of time is a reasonable time to repair or remedy a condition, there is a rebuttable presumption that seven days is a reasonable time. To rebut that presumption, the date on which the landlord received the tenant's notice, the severity and nature of the condition, and the reasonable availability of materials and labor and of utilities from a utility company must be considered.

(e) Except as provided in Subsection (f), a tenant to whom a landlord is liable under Subsection (b) of this section may:

(1) terminate the lease;

(2) have the condition repaired or remedied according to Section 92.0561;

(3) deduct from the tenant's rent, without necessity of judicial action, the cost of the repair or remedy according to Section 92.0561; and

(4) obtain judicial remedies according to Section 92.0563.

(f) A tenant who elects to terminate the lease under Subsection (e) is:

(1) entitled to a pro rata refund of rent from the date of termination or the date the tenant moves out, whichever is later;

(2) entitled to deduct the tenant's security deposit from the tenant's rent without necessity of lawsuit or obtain a refund of the tenant's security deposit according to law; and

(3) not entitled to the other repair and deduct remedies under Section 92.0561 or the judicial remedies under Subdivisions (1) and (2) of Subsection (a) of Section 92.0563.

Sec. 92.0561. Tenant's Repair and Deduct Remedies.

(a) If the landlord is liable to the tenant under Section 92.056(b), the tenant may have the condition repaired or remedied and may deduct the cost from a subsequent rent payment as provided in this section.

(b) The tenant's deduction for the cost of the repair or remedy may not exceed the amount of one month's rent under the lease or $500, whichever is greater. However, if the tenant's rent is subsidized in whole or in part by a governmental agency, the

deduction limitation of one month's rent shall mean the fair market rent for the dwelling and not the rent that the tenant pays. The fair market rent shall be determined by the governmental agency subsidizing the rent, or in the absence of such a determination, it shall be a reasonable amount of rent under the circumstances.

(c) Repairs and deductions under this section may be made as often as necessary so long as the total repairs and deductions in any one month do not exceed one month's rent or $500, whichever is greater.

(d) Repairs under this section may be made only if all of the following requirements are met:

(1) The landlord has a duty to repair or remedy the condition under Section 92.052, and the duty has not been waived in a written lease by the tenant under Subsection (e) or (f) of Section 92.006.

(2) The tenant has given notice to the landlord as required by Section 92.056(b)(1), and, if required, a subsequent notice under Section 92.056(b)(3), and at least one of those notices states that the tenant intends to repair or remedy the condition. The notice shall also contain a reasonable description of the intended repair or remedy.

(3) Any one of the following events has occurred:

(A) The landlord has failed to remedy the backup or overflow of raw sewage inside the tenant's dwelling or the flooding from broken pipes or natural drainage inside the dwelling.

(B) The landlord has expressly or impliedly agreed in the lease to furnish potable water to the tenant's dwelling and the water service to the dwelling has totally ceased.

(C) The landlord has expressly or impliedly agreed in the lease to furnish heating or cooling equipment; the equipment is producing inadequate heat or cooled air; and the landlord has been notified in writing by the appropriate local housing, building, or health official or other official having jurisdiction that the lack of heat or cooling materially affects the health or safety of an ordinary tenant.

(D) The landlord has been notified in writing by the appropriate local housing, building, or health official or other official having jurisdiction that the condition materially affects the health or safety of an ordinary tenant.

(e) If the requirements of Subsection (d) of this section are met, a tenant may:

(1) have the condition repaired or remedied immediately following the tenant's notice of intent to repair if the condition involves sewage or flooding as referred to in Paragraph (A) of Subdivision (3) of Subsection (d) of this section;

(2) have the condition repaired or remedied if the condition involves a cessation of potable water as referred to in Paragraph (A) of Subdivision (3) of Subsection (d) of this section and if the landlord has failed to repair or remedy the condition within three days following the tenant's delivery of notice of intent to repair;

(3) have the condition repaired or remedied if the condition involves inadequate heat or cooled air as referred to in Paragraph (C) of Subdivision (3) of Subsection (d) of this section and if the landlord has failed to repair the condition within three days after delivery of the tenant's notice of intent to repair; or (4) have the condition repaired or remedied if the condition is not covered by Paragraph (A), (B), or (C) of Subdivision (3) of Subsection (d) of this section and involves a condition affecting the physical health or safety of the ordinary tenant as referred to in Paragraph (D) of Subdivision (3) of Subsection (d) of this section and if the landlord has failed to repair or remedy the condition within seven days after delivery of the tenant's notice of intent to repair.

(f) Repairs made pursuant to the tenant's notice must be made by a company, contractor, or repairman listed in the yellow or business pages of the telephone directory or in the classified advertising section of a newspaper of the local city, county, or adjacent county at the time of the tenant's notice of intent to repair. Unless the landlord and tenant agree otherwise under Subsection (g) of this section, repairs may not be made by the tenant, the tenant's immediate family, the tenant's employer or employees, or a company in which the tenant has an ownership interest. Repairs may not be made to the foundation or load-bearing structural elements of the building if it contains two or more dwelling units.

(g) A landlord and a tenant may mutually agree for the tenant to repair or remedy, at the landlord's expense, any condition of the dwelling regardless of whether it materially affects the health or safety of an ordinary tenant. However, the landlord's duty to repair or remedy conditions covered by this subchapter may not be waived except as provided by Subsection (e) or (f) of Section 92.006.

(h) Repairs made pursuant to the tenant's notice must be made in compliance with applicable building codes, including a building permit when required.

(i) The tenant shall not have authority to contract for labor or materials in excess of what the tenant may deduct under this section. The landlord is not liable to repairmen, contractors, or material suppliers who furnish labor or materials to repair or remedy the condition. A repairman or supplier shall not have a lien for materials or services arising out of repairs contracted for by the tenant under this section.

(j) When deducting the cost of repairs from the rent payment, the tenant shall furnish the landlord, along with payment of the balance of the rent, a copy of the repair bill and the receipt for its payment. A repair bill and receipt may be the same document.

(k) If the landlord repairs or remedies the condition or delivers an affidavit for delay under Section 92.0562 to the tenant after the tenant has contacted a repairman but before the repairman commences work, the landlord shall be liable for the cost incurred by the tenant for the repairman's trip charge, and the tenant may deduct the charge from the tenant's rent as if it were a repair cost.

Sec. 92.0562. Landlord Affidavit for Delay.

(a) The tenant must delay contracting for repairs under Section 92.0561 if, before the tenant contracts for the repairs, the landlord delivers to the tenant an affidavit, signed and sworn to under oath by the landlord or his authorized agent and complying with this section.

(b) The affidavit must summarize the reasons for the delay and the diligent efforts made by the landlord up to the date of the affidavit to get the repairs done. The affidavit must state facts showing that the landlord has made and is making diligent efforts to repair the condition, and it must contain dates, names, addresses, and telephone numbers of contractors, suppliers, and repairmen contacted by the owner.

(c) Affidavits under this section may delay repair by the tenant for:

(1) 15 days if the landlord's failure to repair is caused by a delay in obtaining necessary parts for which the landlord is not at fault; or

(2) 30 days if the landlord's failure to repair is caused by a general shortage of labor or materials for repair following a natural disaster such as a hurricane, tornado, flood, extended freeze, or widespread windstorm.

(d) Affidavits for delay based on grounds other than those listed in Subsection (c) of this section are unlawful, and if used, they are of no effect. The landlord may file subsequent affidavits, provided that the total delay of the repair or remedy extends no longer than six months from the date the landlord delivers the first affidavit to the tenant.

(e) The affidavit must be delivered to the tenant by any of the following methods:

(1) personal delivery to the tenant;

(2) certified mail, return receipt requested, to the tenant; or

(3) leaving the notice inside the dwelling in a conspicuous place if notice in that manner is authorized in a written lease.

(f) Affidavits for delay by a landlord under this section must be submitted in good faith. Following delivery of the affidavit, the landlord must continue diligent efforts to repair or remedy the condition. There shall be a rebuttable presumption that the landlord acted in good faith and with continued diligence for the first affidavit for delay the landlord delivers to the tenant. The landlord shall have the burden of pleading and proving good faith and continued diligence for subsequent affidavits for delay. A landlord who violates this section shall be liable to the tenant for all judicial remedies under Section 92.0563 except that the civil penalty under Subdivision (3) of Subsection (a) of Section 92.0563 shall be one month's rent plus $1,000.

(g) If the landlord is liable to the tenant under Section 92.056 and if a new landlord, in good faith and without knowledge of the tenant's notice of intent to repair, has acquired title to the tenant's dwelling by foreclosure, deed in lieu of foreclosure, or general warranty deed in a bona fide purchase, then the following shall apply:

(1) The tenant's right to terminate the lease under this subchapter shall not be affected, and the tenant shall have no duty to give additional notice to the new landlord.

(2) The tenant's right to repair and deduct for conditions involving sewage backup or overflow, flooding inside the dwelling, or a cutoff of potable water under Subsection (e) of Section 92.0561 shall not be affected, and the tenant shall have no duty to give additional notice to the new landlord.

(3) For conditions other than those specified in Subdivision (2) of this subsection, if the new landlord acquires title as described in this subsection and has notified the tenant of the name and address of the new landlord or the new landlord's authorized agent and if the tenant has not already contracted for the repair or remedy at the time the tenant is so notified, the tenant must deliver to the new landlord a written notice of intent to repair or remedy the condition, and the new landlord shall have a reasonable time to complete the repair before the tenant may repair or remedy the condition. No further notice from the tenant is necessary in order for the tenant to repair or remedy the condition after a reasonable time has elapsed.

(4) The tenant's judicial remedies under Section 92.0563 shall be limited to recovery against the landlord to whom the tenant gave the required notices until the tenant has given the new landlord the notices required by this section and otherwise complied with Section 92.056 as to the new landlord.

(5) If the new landlord violates this subsection, the new landlord is liable to the tenant for a civil penalty of one month's rent plus $2,000, actual damages, and attorney's fees.

(6) No provision of this section shall affect any right of a foreclosing superior lienholder to terminate, according to law, any interest in the premises held by the holders of subordinate liens, encumbrances, leases, or other interests and shall not affect any right of the tenant to terminate the lease according to law.

Sec. 92.0563. Tenant's Judicial Remedies.

(a) A tenant's judicial remedies under Section 92.056 shall include:

(1) an order directing the landlord to take reasonable action to repair or remedy the condition;

(2) an order reducing the tenant's rent, from the date of the first repair notice, in proportion to the reduced rental value resulting from the condition until the condition is repaired or remedied;

(3) a judgment against the landlord for a civil penalty of one month's rent plus $500;

(4) a judgment against the landlord for the amount of the tenant's actual damages; and

(5) court costs and attorney's fees, excluding any attorney's fees for a cause of action for damages relating to a personal injury.

(b) A landlord who knowingly violates Section 92.006 by contracting orally or in writing with a tenant to waive the landlord's duty to repair under this subchapter shall be liable to the tenant for actual damages, a civil penalty of one month's rent plus $2,000, and reasonable attorney's fees. For purposes of this subsection, there shall be a rebuttable presumption that the landlord acted without knowledge of the violation. The tenant shall have the burden of pleading and proving a knowing violation. If the lease is in writing and is not in violation of Section 92.006, the tenant's proof of a knowing violation must be clear and convincing. A mutual agreement for tenant repair under Subsection (g) of Section 92.0561 is not a violation of Section 92.006.

(c) The justice, county, and district courts have concurrent jurisdiction of an action under Subsection (a) of this section except that the justice court may not order repairs under Subdivision (1) of Subsection (a) of this section.

Sec. 92.058. Landlord Remedy for Tenant Violation.

(a) If the tenant withholds rents, causes repairs to be performed, or makes rent deductions for repairs in violation of this subchapter, the landlord may recover actual damages from the tenant. If, after a landlord has notified a tenant in writing of (1) the illegality of the tenant's rent withholding or the tenant's proposed repair and (2) the penalties of this subchapter, the tenant withholds rent, causes repairs to be performed, or makes rent deductions for repairs in bad faith violation of this subchapter, the landlord may recover from the tenant a civil penalty of one month's rent plus $500.

(b) Notice under this section must be in writing and may be given in person, by mail, or by delivery to the premises.

(c) The landlord has the burden of pleading and proving, by clear and convincing evidence, that the landlord gave the tenant the required notice of the illegality and the penalties and that the tenant's violation was done in bad faith. In any litigation under this subsection, the prevailing party shall recover reasonable attorney's fees from the nonprevailing party.

Sec. 92.060. Agents for Delivery of Notice.

A managing agent, leasing agent, or resident manager is the agent of the landlord for purposes of notice and other communications required or permitted by this subchapter.

Sec. 92.061. Effect on Other Rights.

The duties of a landlord and the remedies of a tenant under this subchapter are in lieu of existing common law and other statutory law warranties and duties of landlords for maintenance, repair, security, habitability, and nonretaliation, and remedies of tenants for a violation of those warranties and duties. Otherwise, this subchapter does not affect any other right of a landlord or tenant under contract, statutory law, or common law that is consistent with the purposes of this subchapter or any right a landlord or tenant may have to bring an action for personal injury or property damage under the law of this state. This subchapter does not impose obligations on a landlord or tenant other than those expressly stated in this subchapter.

SUBCHAPTER C. SECURITY DEPOSITS

Sec. 92.101. Application.

This subchapter applies to all residential leases.

Sec. 92.102. Security Deposit.

A security deposit is any advance of money, other than a rental application deposit or an advance payment of rent, that is intended primarily to secure performance under a lease of a dwelling that has been entered into by a landlord and a tenant.

Sec. 92.103. Obligation to Refund.

(a) Except as provided by Section 92.107, the landlord shall refund a security deposit to the tenant on or before the 30th day after the date the tenant surrenders the premises.

(b) A requirement that a tenant give advance notice of surrender as a condition for refunding the security deposit is effective only if the requirement is underlined or is printed in conspicuous bold print in the lease.

(c) The tenant's claim to the security deposit takes priority over the claim of any creditor of the landlord, including a trustee in bankruptcy.

Sec. 92.1031. Conditions for Retention of Security Deposit or Rent Prepayment.

(a) Except as provided in Subsection (b), a landlord who receives a security deposit or rent prepayment for a dwelling from a tenant who fails to occupy the dwelling according to a lease between the landlord and the tenant may not retain the security deposit or rent prepayment if:

(1) the tenant secures a replacement tenant satisfactory to the landlord and the replacement tenant occupies the dwelling on or before the commencement date of the lease; or

(2) the landlord secures a replacement tenant satisfactory to the landlord and the replacement tenant occupies the dwelling on or before the commencement date of the lease.

(b) If the landlord secures the replacement tenant, the landlord may retain and deduct from the security deposit or rent prepayment either:

(1) a sum agreed to in the lease as a lease cancellation fee; or

(2) actual expenses incurred by the landlord in securing the replacement, including a reasonable amount for the time of the landlord in securing the replacement tenant.

Sec. 92.104. Retention of Security Deposit; Accounting.

(a) Before returning a security deposit, the landlord may deduct from the deposit damages and charges for which the tenant is legally liable under the lease or as a result of breaching the lease.

(b) The landlord may not retain any portion of a security deposit to cover normal wear and tear.

(c) If the landlord retains all or part of a security deposit under this section, the landlord shall give to the tenant the balance of the security deposit, if any, together with a written description and itemized list of all deductions. The landlord is not required to give the tenant a description and itemized list of deductions if:

(1) the tenant owes rent when he surrenders possession of the premises; and

(2) there is no controversy concerning the amount of rent owed.

Sec. 92.1041. Presumption of Refund or Accounting.

A landlord is presumed to have refunded a security deposit or made an accounting of security deposit deductions if, on or before the date required under this subchapter, the refund or accounting is placed in the United States mail and postmarked on or before the required date.

Sec. 92.105. Cessation of Owner's Interest.

(a) If the owner's interest in the premises is terminated by sale, assignment, death, appointment of a receiver, bankruptcy, or otherwise, the new owner is liable for the return of security deposits according to this subchapter from the date title to the premises is acquired, regardless of whether notice is given to the tenant under Subsection (b) of this section.

(b) The person who no longer owns an interest in the rental premises remains liable for a security deposit received while the person was the owner until the new owner delivers to the tenant a signed statement acknowledging that the new owner has received and is responsible for the tenant's security deposit and specifying the exact dollar amount of the deposit.

(c) Subsection (a) does not apply to a real estate mortgage lienholder who acquires title by foreclosure.

Sec. 92.106. Records.

The landlord shall keep accurate records of all security deposits.

Sec. 92.107. Tenant's Forwarding Address.

(a) The landlord is not obligated to return a tenant's security deposit or give the tenant a written description of damages and charges until the tenant gives the landlord a written statement of the tenant's forwarding address for the purpose of refunding the security deposit.

(b) The tenant does not forfeit the right to a refund of the security deposit or the right to receive a description of damages and charges merely for failing to give a forwarding address to the landlord.

Sec. 92.108. Liability for Withholding Last Month's Rent.

(a) The tenant may not withhold payment of any portion of the last month's rent on grounds that the security deposit is security for unpaid rent.

(b) A tenant who violates this section is presumed to have acted in bad faith. A tenant who in bad faith violates this section is liable to the landlord for an amount equal to three times the rent wrongfully withheld and the landlord's reasonable attorney's fees in a suit to recover the rent.

Sec. 92.109. Liability of Landlord.

(a) A landlord who in bad faith retains a security deposit in violation of this subchapter is liable for an amount equal to the sum of $100, three times the portion of the deposit wrongfully withheld, and the tenant's reasonable attorney's fees in a suit to recover the deposit.

(b) A landlord who in bad faith does not provide a written description and itemized list of damages and charges in violation of this subchapter:

(1) forfeits the right to withhold any portion of the security deposit or to bring suit against the tenant for damages to the premises; and

(2) is liable for the tenant's reasonable attorney's fees in a suit to recover the deposit.

(c) In an action brought by a tenant under this subchapter, the landlord has the burden of proving that the retention of any portion of the security deposit was reasonable.

(d) A landlord who fails either to return a security deposit or to provide a written description and itemization of deductions on or before the 30th day after the date the tenant surrenders possession is presumed to have acted in bad faith.

SUBCHAPTER D. SECURITY DEVICES

Sec. 92.151. Definitions.

In this subchapter:

(1) "Doorknob lock" means a lock in a doorknob, with the lock operated from the exterior by a key, card, or combination and from the interior without a key, card, or combination.

(2) "Door viewer" means a permanently installed device in an exterior door that allows a person inside the dwelling to view a person outside the door. The device must be:

(A) a clear glass pane or one-way mirror; or

(B) a peephole having a barrel with a one-way lens of glass or other substance providing an angle view of not less than 160 degrees.

(3) "Exterior door" means a door providing access from a dwelling interior to the exterior. The term includes a door between a living area and a garage but does not include a sliding glass door or a screen door.

(4) "French doors" means a set of two exterior doors in which each door is hinged and abuts the other door when closed. The term includes double-hinged patio doors.

(5) "Keyed dead bolt" means:

(A) a door lock not in the doorknob that:

(i) locks with a bolt into the doorjamb; and

(ii) is operated from the exterior by a key, card, or combination and from the interior by a knob or lever without a key, card, or combination; or

(B) a doorknob lock that contains a bolt with at least a one-inch throw.

(6) "Keyless bolting device" means a door lock not in the doorknob that locks:

(A) with a bolt into a strike plate screwed into the portion of the doorjamb surface that faces the edge of the door when the door is closed or into a metal doorjamb that serves as the strike plate, operable only by knob or lever from the door's interior and not in any manner from the door's exterior, and that is commonly known as a keyless dead bolt;

(B) by a drop bolt system operated by placing a central metal plate over a metal doorjamb restraint that protrudes from the doorjamb and that is affixed to the doorjamb frame by means of three case-hardened screws at least three inches in length. One-half of the central plate must overlap the interior surface of the door and the other half of the central plate must overlap the doorjamb when the plate is placed over the doorjamb restraint. The drop bolt system must prevent the door from being opened unless the central plate is lifted off of the doorjamb restraint by a person who is on the interior side of the door.

The term "keyless bolting device" does not include a chain latch, flip latch, surface-mounted slide bolt, mortise door bolt, surface-mounted barrel bolt, surface-mounted swing bar door guard, spring-loaded nightlatch, foot bolt, or other lock or latch; or

(C) by a metal bar or metal tube that is placed across the entire interior side of the door and secured in place at each end of the bar or tube by heavy-duty metal screw hooks. The screw hooks must be at least three inches in length and must be screwed into the door frame stud or wall stud on each side of the door. The bar or tube must be capable of being secured to both of the screw hooks and must be permanently attached in some way to the door frame stud or wall stud. When secured to the screw hooks, the bar or tube must prevent the door from being opened unless the bar or tube is removed by a person who is on the interior side of the door.

(7) "Landlord" means a dwelling owner, lessor, sublessor, management company, or managing agent, including an on-site manager.

(8) "Multiunit complex" means two or more dwellings in one or more buildings that are:

(A) under common ownership;

(B) managed by the same owner, agent, or management company; and

(C) located on the same lot or tract or adjacent lots or tracts of land.

(9) "Possession of a dwelling" means occupancy by a tenant under a lease, including occupancy until the time the tenant moves out or a writ of possession is issued by a court. The term does not include occupancy before the initial occupancy date authorized under a lease.

(10) "Rekey" means to change or alter a security device that is operated by a key, card, or combination so that a different key, card, or combination is necessary to operate the security device.

(11) "Security device" means a doorknob lock, door viewer, keyed dead bolt, keyless bolting device, sliding door handle latch sliding door pin lock, sliding door security bar, or window latch in a dwelling.

(12) "Sliding door handle latch" means a latch or lock:

(A) located near the handle on a sliding glass door;

(B) operated with or without a key; and

(C) designed to prevent the door from being opened.

(13) "Sliding door pin lock" means a lock on a sliding glass door that consists of a pin or nail inserted from the interior side of the door at the side opposite the door's handle and that is designed to prevent the door from being opened or lifted.

(14) "Sliding door security bar" means a bar or rod that can be placed at the bottom of or across the interior side of the fixed panel of a sliding glass door and that is designed to prevent the door from being opened.

(15) "Tenant turnover date" means the date a new tenant moves into a dwelling under a lease after all previous tenants have moved out. The term does not include dates of entry or occupation not authorized by the landlord.

(16) "Window latch" means a device on a window that prevents the window from being opened and that is operated without a key and only from the interior.

Sec. 92.152. Application of Subchapter.

(a) This subchapter does not apply to:

(1) room in a hotel, motel, or inn or to similar transient housing;

(2) residential housing owned or operated by a public or private college or university accredited by a recognized accrediting agency as defined under Section 61.003, Education Code;

(3) residential housing operated by preparatory schools accredited by the Texas Education Agency, a regional accrediting agency, or any accrediting agency recognized by the commissioner of education; or

(4) a temporary residential tenancy created by a contract for sale in which the buyer occupies the property before closing or the seller occupies the property after closing for a specific term not to exceed 90 days.

(b) Except as provided by Subsection (a), a dwelling to which this subchapter applies includes:

(1) a room in a dormitory or rooming house;

(2) a mobile home;

(3) a single family house, duplex, or triplex; and

(4) a living unit in an apartment, condominium, cooperative, or townhome project.

Sec. 92.153. Security Devices Required Without Necessity of Tenant Request.

(a) Except as provided by Subsections (b), (e), (f), (g), and (h) and without necessity of request by the tenant, a dwelling must be equipped with:

(1) a window latch on each exterior window of the dwelling;

(2) a doorknob lock or keyed dead bolt on each exterior door;

(3) a sliding door pin lock on each exterior sliding glass door of the dwelling;

(4) a sliding door handle latch or a sliding door security bar on each exterior sliding glass door of the dwelling; and

(5) a keyless bolting device and a door viewer on each exterior door of the dwelling.

(b) If the dwelling has French doors, one door of each pair of French doors must meet the requirements of Subsection (a) and the other door must have:

(1) a keyed dead bolt or keyless bolting device capable of insertion into the doorjamb above the door and a keyless bolting device capable of insertion into the floor or threshold, each with a bolt having a throw of one inch or more; or

(2) a bolt installed inside the door and operated from the edge of the door, capable of insertion into the doorjamb above the door, and another bolt installed inside the door and operated from the edge of the door capable of insertion into the floor or threshold, each bolt having a throw of three-fourths inch or more.

(c) A security device required by Subsection (a) or (b) must be installed at the landlord's expense.

(d) Subsections (a) and (b) apply only when a tenant is in possession of a dwelling.

(e) A keyless bolting device is not required to be installed at the landlord's expense on an exterior door if:

(1) the dwelling is part of a multiunit complex in which the majority of dwelling units are leased to tenants who are over 55 years of age or who have a physical or mental disability;

(2) a tenant or occupant in the dwelling is over 55 years of age or has a physical or mental disability; and

(3) the landlord is expressly required or permitted to periodically check on the well-being or health of the tenant as a part of a written lease or other written agreement.

(f) A keyless bolting device is not required to be installed at the landlord's expense if a tenant or occupant in the dwelling is over 55 years of age or has a physical or mental disability, the tenant requests, in writing, that the landlord deactivate or not install the keyless bolting device, and the tenant certifies in the request that the tenant or occupant is over 55 years of age or has a physical or mental disability. The request must be a separate document and may not be included as part of a lease agreement. A landlord is not exempt as provided by this subsection if the landlord knows or has reason to know that the requirements of this subsection are not fulfilled.

(g) A keyed dead bolt or a doorknob lock is not required to be installed at the landlord's expense on an exterior door if at the time the tenant agrees to lease the dwelling:

(1) at least one exterior door usable for normal entry into the dwelling has both a keyed dead bolt and a keyless bolting device, installed in accordance with the height, strike plate, and throw requirements of Section 92.154; and

(2) all other exterior doors have a keyless bolting device installed in accordance with the height, strike plate, and throw requirements of Section 92.154.

(h) A security device required by this section must be operable throughout the time a tenant is in possession of a dwelling. However, a landlord may deactivate or remove the locking mechanism of a doorknob lock or remove any device not qualifying as a keyless bolting device if a keyed dead bolt has been installed on the same door.

(i) A landlord is subject to the tenant remedies provided by Section 92.164(a)(4) if the landlord:

(1) deactivates or does not install a keyless bolting device, claiming an exemption under Subsection (e), (f), or (g); and

(2) knows or has reason to know that the requirements of the subsection granting the exemption are not fulfilled.

Sec. 92.154. Height, Strike Plate, and Throw Requirements--Keyed Dead Bolt or Keyless Bolting Device.

(a) A keyed dead bolt or a keyless bolting device required by this subchapter must be installed at a height:

(1) not lower than 36 inches from the floor; and

(2) not higher than:

    (A) 54 inches from the floor, if installed before September 1, 1993; or

    (B) 48 inches from the floor, if installed on or after September 1, 1993.

(b) A keyed dead bolt or a keyless bolting device described in Section 92.151(6)(A) or (B) in a dwelling must:

(1) have a strike plate screwed into the portion of the doorjamb surface that faces the edge of the door when the door is closed; or

(2) be installed in a door with a metal doorjamb that serves as the strike plate.

(c) A keyed dead bolt or keyless dead bolt, as described by Section 92.151(6)(A), installed in a dwelling on or after September 1, 1993, must have a bolt with a throw of not less than one inch.

(d) The requirements of this section do not apply to a keyed dead bolt or a keyless bolting device in one door of a pair of French doors that is installed in accordance with the requirements of Section 92.153(b)(1) or (2).

Sec. 92.155. Height Requirements--Sliding Door Security Devices.

A sliding door pin lock or sliding door security bar required by this subchapter must be installed at a height not higher than:

(1) 54 inches from the floor, if installed before September 1, 1993; or

(2) 48 inches from the floor, if installed on or after September 1, 1993.

Sec. 92.156. Rekeying or Change of Security Devices.

(a) A security device operated by a key, card, or combination shall be rekeyed by the landlord at the landlord's expense not later than the seventh day after each tenant turnover date.

(b) A landlord shall perform additional rekeying or change a security device at the tenant's expense if requested by the tenant. A tenant may make an unlimited number of requests under this subsection.

(c) The expense of rekeying security devices for purposes of the use or change of the landlord's master key must be paid by the landlord.

(d) This section does not apply to locks on closet doors or other interior doors.

Sec. 92.157. Security Devices Requested by Tenant.

(a) At a tenant's request made at any time, a landlord, at the tenant's expense, shall install:

(1) a keyed dead bolt on an exterior door if the door has:

    (A) a doorknob lock but not a keyed dead bolt; or

    (B) a keyless bolting device but not a keyed dead bolt or doorknob lock; and

(2) a sliding door pin lock or sliding door security bar if the door is an exterior sliding glass door without a sliding door pin lock or sliding door security bar.

(b) At a tenant's request made before January 1, 1995, a landlord, at the tenant's expense, shall install on an exterior door of a dwelling constructed before September 1, 1993:

(1) a keyless bolting device if the door does not have a keyless bolting device; and

(2) a door viewer if the door does not have a door viewer.

(c) If a security device required by Section 92.153 to be installed on or after January 1, 1995, without necessity of a tenant's request has not been installed by the landlord, the tenant may request the landlord to immediately install it, and the landlord shall immediately install it at the landlord's expense.

Sec. 92.158. Landlord's Defenses.

The landlord has a defense to liability under Section 92.156 if:

(1) the tenant has not fully paid all rent then due from the tenant on the date the tenant gives a request under Subsection (a) of Section 92.153 or the notice required by Section 92.156; or

(2) on the date the tenant terminates the lease or files suit the tenant has not fully paid costs requested by the landlord and authorized by Section 92.154.

Sec. 92.158.* Landlord's Duty to Repair or Replace Security Device.

During the lease term and any renewal period, a landlord shall repair or replace a security device on request or notification by the tenant that the security device is inoperable or in need of repair or replacement.

* *Note:* This is not a typographical error. The Texas Legislature has duplicated section number 92.158.

Sec. 92.159. When Tenant's Request or Notice Must be in Writing.

A tenant's request or notice under this subchapter may be given orally unless the tenant has a written lease that requires the request or notice to be in writing and that requirement is underlined or in boldfaced print in the lease.

Sec. 92.160. Type, Brand, and Manner of Installation.

Except as otherwise required by this subchapter, a landlord may select the type, brand, and manner of installation, including placement, of a security device installed under this subchapter. This section does not apply to a security device installed, repaired, changed, replaced, or rekeyed by a tenant under Section 92.164(a)(1) or 92.165(1).

Sec. 92.161. Compliance With Tenant Request Required Within Reasonable Time.

(a) Except as provided by Subsections (b) and (c), a landlord must comply with a tenant's request for rekeying, changing, installing, repairing, or replacing a security device under Section 92.156, 92.157, or 92.158 within a reasonable time. A reasonable time for purposes of this subsection is presumed to be not later than the seventh day after the date the request is received by the landlord.

(b) If within the time allowed under Section 92.162(c) a landlord requests advance payment of charges that the landlord is entitled to collect under that section, the landlord shall comply with a tenant's request under Section 92.156(b), 92.157(a), or 92.157(b) within a reasonable time. A reasonable time for purposes of this subsection is presumed to be not later than the seventh day after the date a tenant's advance payment is received by the landlord, except as provided by Subsection (c).

(c) A reasonable time for purposes of Subsections (a) and (b) is presumed to be not later than 72 hours after the time of receipt of the tenant's request and any required advance payment if at the time of making the request the tenant informed the landlord that:

(1) an unauthorized entry occurred or was attempted in the tenant's dwelling;

(2) an unauthorized entry occurred or was attempted in another unit in the multiunit complex in which the tenant's dwelling is located during the two months preceding the date of the request; or

(3) a crime of personal violence occurred in the multiunit complex in which the tenant's dwelling is located during the two months preceding the date of the request.

(d) A landlord may rebut the presumption provided by Subsection (a) or (b) if despite the diligence of the landlord:

(1) the landlord did not know of the tenant's request, without the fault of the landlord;

(2) materials, labor, or utilities were unavailable; or

(3) a delay was caused by circumstances beyond the landlord's control, including the illness or death of the landlord or a member of the landlord's immediate family.

(e) This section does not apply to a landlord's duty to install or rekey, without necessity of a tenant's request, a security device under Section 92.153 or 92.156(a).

Sec. 92.162. Payment of Charges; Limits on Amount Charged.

(a) A landlord may not require a tenant to pay for repair or replacement of a security device due to normal wear and tear. A landlord may not require a tenant to pay for other repairs or replacements of a security device except as provided by Subsections (b), (c), and (d).

(b) A landlord may require a tenant to pay for repair or replacement of a security device if an underlined provision in a written lease authorizes the landlord to do so and the repair or replacement is necessitated by misuse or damage by the tenant, a member of the tenant's family, an occupant, or a guest, and not by normal wear and tear. Misuse of or damage to a security device that occurs during the tenant's occupancy is presumed to be caused by the tenant, a family member, an occupant, or a guest. The tenant has the burden of proving that the misuse or damage was caused by another party.

(c) A landlord may require a tenant to pay in advance charges for which the tenant is liable under this subchapter if a written lease authorizes the landlord to require advance payment, and the landlord notifies the tenant within a reasonable time after the tenant's request that advance payment is required, and:

(1) the tenant is more than 30 days delinquent in reimbursing the landlord for charges to which the landlord is entitled under Subsection (b); or

(2) the tenant requested that the landlord repair, install, change, or rekey the same security device during the 30 days preceding the tenant's request, and the landlord complied with the request.

(d) A landlord authorized by this subchapter to charge a tenant for repairing, installing, changing, or rekeying a security device under this subchapter may not require the tenant to pay more than the total cost charged by a third-party contractor for material, labor, taxes, and extra keys. If the landlord's employees perform the work, the charge may include a reasonable amount for overhead but may not include a profit to the landlord. If management company employees perform the work, the charge may include reasonable overhead and profit but may not exceed the cost charged to the owner by the management company for comparable security devices installed by management company employees at the owner's request and expense.

(e) The owner of a dwelling shall reimburse a management company, managing agent, or on-site manager for costs expended by that person in complying with this subchapter. A management company, managing agent, or on-site manager may reimburse itself for the costs from the owner's funds in its possession or control.

Sec. 92.163. Removal or Alteration of Security Device by Tenant.

A security device that is installed, changed, or rekeyed under this subchapter becomes a fixture of the dwelling. Except as provided by Section 92.164(a)(1) or 92.165(1) regarding the remedy of repair-and-deduct, a tenant may not remove, change, rekey, replace, or alter a security device or have it removed, changed, rekeyed, replaced, or altered without permission of the landlord.

Sec. 92.164. Tenant Remedies for Landlord's Failure to Install or Rekey Certain Security Devices.

(a) If a landlord does not comply with Section 92.153 or 92.156(a) regarding installation or rekeying of a security device, the tenant may:

(1) install or rekey the security device as required

by this subchapter and deduct the reasonable cost of material, labor, taxes, and extra keys from the tenant's next rent payment, in accordance with Section 92.166;

(2) serve a written request for compliance on the landlord, and, except as provided by Subsections (b) and (c), if the landlord does not comply on or before the third day after the date the notice is received, unilaterally terminate the lease without court proceedings;

(3) file suit against the landlord without serving a request for compliance and obtain a judgment for:

(A) a court order directing the landlord to comply, if the tenant is in possession of the dwelling;

(B) the tenant's actual damages;

(C) court costs; and

(D) attorney's fees except in suits for recovery of property damages, personal injuries, or wrongful death; and

(4) serve a written request for compliance on the landlord, and, except as provided by Subsections (b) and (c), if the landlord does not comply on or before the third day after the date the notice is received, file suit against the landlord and obtain a judgment for:

(A) a court order directing the landlord to comply and bring all dwellings owned by the landlord into compliance, if the tenant serving the written request is in possession of the dwelling;

(B) the tenant's actual damages;

(C) punitive damages if the tenant suffers actual damages;

(D) a civil penalty of one month's rent plus $500;

(E) court costs; and

(F) attorney's fees except in suits for recovery of property damages, personal injuries, or wrongful death.

(b) A tenant may not unilaterally terminate the lease under Subsection (a)(2) or file suit against the landlord to obtain a judgment under Subsection (a)(4) unless the landlord does not comply on or before the seventh day after the date the written request for compliance is received if the lease includes language underlined or in boldface print that in substance provides the tenant with notice that:

(1) the landlord at the landlord's expense is required to equip the dwelling, when the tenant takes possession, with the security devices described by Sections 92.153(a)(1)-(4) and (6);

(2) the landlord is not required to install a doorknob lock or keyed dead bolt at the landlord's expense if the exterior doors meet the requirements of Section 92.153(f);

(3) the landlord is not required to install a keyless bolting device at the landlord's expense on an exterior door if the landlord is expressly required or permitted to periodically check on the well-being or health of the tenant as provided by Section 92.153(e)(3); and

(4) the tenant has the right to install or rekey a security device required by this subchapter and deduct the reasonable cost from the tenant's next rent payment, as provided by Subsection (a)(1).

(c) Regardless of whether the lease contains language complying with the requirements of Subsection (b), the additional time for landlord compliance provided by Subsection (b) does not apply if at the time the tenant served the written request for compliance on the landlord the tenant informed the landlord that an unauthorized entry occurred or was attempted in the tenant's dwelling, an unauthorized entry occurred or was attempted in another unit in the multiunit complex in which the tenant's dwelling is located during the two months preceding the date of the request, or a crime of personal violence occurred in the multiunit complex in which the tenant's dwelling is located during the two months preceding the date of the request, unless despite the diligence of the landlord:

(1) the landlord did not know of the tenant's request, without the fault of the landlord;

(2) materials, labor, or utilities were unavailable; or

(3) a delay was caused by circumstances beyond the landlord's control, including the illness or death of the landlord or a member of the landlord's immediate family.

Sec. 92.165. Tenant Remedies for Other Landlord Violations.

If a landlord does not comply with a tenant's request regarding rekeying, changing, adding, repairing, or replacing a security device under Section 92.156(b), 92.157, or 92.158 in accordance

with the time limits and other requirements of this subchapter, the tenant may:

(1) install, repair, change, replace, or rekey the security devices as required by this subchapter and deduct the reasonable cost of material, labor, taxes, and extra keys from the tenant's next rent payment in accordance with Section 92.166;

(2) unilaterally terminate the lease without court proceedings; and

(3) file suit against the landlord and obtain a judgment for:

(A) a court order directing the landlord to comply, if the tenant is in possession of the dwelling;

(B) the tenant's actual damages;

(C) punitive damages if the tenant suffers actual damages and the landlord's failure to comply is intentional, malicious, or grossly negligent;

(D) a civil penalty of one month's rent plus $500;

(E) court costs; and

(F) attorney's fees except in suits for recovery of property damages, personal injuries, or wrongful death.

Sec. 92.166. Notice of Tenant's Deduction of Repair Costs From Rent.

(a) A tenant shall notify the landlord of a rent deduction attributable to the tenant's installing, repairing, changing, replacing, or rekeying of a security device under Section 92.164(a)(1) or 92.165(1) after the landlord's failure to comply with this subchapter. The notice must be given at the time of the reduced rent payment.

(b) Unless otherwise provided in a written lease, a tenant shall provide one duplicate of the key to any key-operated security device installed or rekeyed by the tenant under Section 92.164(a)(1) or 92.165(1) within a reasonable time after the landlord's written request for the key.

Sec. 92.167. Landlord's Defenses.

(a) A landlord has a defense to liability under Section 92.165 if on the date the tenant terminates the lease or files suit the tenant has not fully paid costs requested by the landlord and authorized by this subchapter.

(b) A management company or managing agent who is not the owner of a dwelling and who has not purported to be the owner in the lease has a defense to liability under Sections 92.164 and 92.165 if before the date the tenant is in possession of the dwelling or the date of the tenant's request for installation, repair, replacement, change, or rekeying and before any property damage or personal injury to the tenant, the management company or managing agent:

(1) did not have funds of the dwelling owner in its possession or control with which to comply with this subchapter;

(2) made written request to the dwelling owner that the owner fund and allow installation, repair, change, replacement, or rekeying of security devices as required under this subchapter and mailed the request, certified mail return receipt requested, to the dwelling owner; and

(3) not later than the third day after the date of receipt of the tenant's request, provided the tenant with a written notice:

(A) stating that the management company or managing agent has taken the actions in Subdivisions (1) and (2);

(B) stating that the owner has not provided or will not provide the necessary funds; and

(C) explaining the remedies available to the tenant for the landlord's failure to comply.

Sec. 92.168. Tenant's Remedy on Notice From Management Company.

The tenant may unilaterally terminate the lease or exercise other remedies under Sections 92.164 and 92.165 after receiving written notice from a management company that the owner of the dwelling has not provided or will not provide funds to repair, install, change, replace, or rekey a security device as required by this subchapter.

Sec. 92.169. Agent for Delivery of Notice.

A managing agent or an agent to whom rent is regularly paid, whether residing or maintaining an office on-site or off-site, is the agent of the landlord for purposes of notice and other communications required or permitted by this subchapter.

Sec. 92.170. Effect on Other Landlord Duties and Tenant Remedies.

The duties of a landlord and the remedies of a tenant under this subchapter are in lieu of common law, other statutory law, and local ordinances relating to a residential landlord's duty to install, change,

rekey, repair, or replace security devices and a tenant's remedies for the landlord's failure to install, change, rekey, repair, or replace security devices, except that a municipal ordinance adopted before January 1, 1993, may require installation of security devices at the landlord's expense by an earlier date than a date required by this subchapter. This subchapter does not affect a duty of a landlord or a remedy of a tenant under Subchapter B regarding habitability.

SUBCHAPTER E. DISCLOSURE OF OWNERSHIP AND MANAGEMENT

Sec. 92.201. Disclosure of Ownership and Management.

(a) A landlord shall disclose to a tenant, or to any government official or employee acting in an official capacity, according to this subchapter:

(1) the name and either a street or post office box address of the holder of record title, according to the deed records in the county clerk's office, of the dwelling rented by the tenant or inquired about by the government official or employee acting in an official capacity; and

(2) if an entity located off-site from the dwelling is primarily responsible for managing the dwelling, the name and street address of the management company.

(b) Disclosure to a tenant under Subsection (a) must be made by:

(1) giving the information in writing to the tenant on or before the seventh day after the day the landlord receives the tenant's request for the information;

(2) continuously posting the information in a conspicuous place in the dwelling or the office of the on-site manager or on the outside of the entry door to the office of the on-site manager on or before the seventh day after the date the landlord receives the tenant's request for the information; or

(3) including the information in a copy of the tenant's lease or in written rules given to the tenant before the tenant requests the information.

(c) Disclosure of information to a tenant may be made under Subdivision (1) or (2) of Subsection (b) before the tenant requests the information.

(d) Disclosure of information to a government official or employee must be made by giving the information in writing to the official or employee on or before the seventh day after the date the landlord receives the request from the official or employee for the information.

(e) A correction to the information may be made by any of the methods authorized for providing the information.

(f) For the purposes of this section, an owner or property manager may disclose either an actual name or names or an assumed name if an assumed name certificate has been recorded with the county clerk.

Sec. 92.202. Landlord's Failure to Disclose Information.

(a) A landlord is liable to a tenant or a governmental body according to this subchapter if:

(1) after the tenant or government official or employee makes a request for information under Section 92.201, the landlord does not provide the information; and

(2) the landlord does not give the information to the tenant or government official or employee before the eighth day after the date the tenant, official, or employee gives the landlord written notice that the tenant, official, or employee may exercise remedies under this subchapter if the landlord does not comply with the request by the tenant, official, or employee for the information within seven days.

(b) If the tenant's lease is in writing, the lease may require the tenant's initial request for information to be written. A request by a government official or employee for information must be in writing.

Sec. 92.203. Landlord's Failure to Correct Information.

A landlord who has provided information under Subdivision (2) or (3) of Subsection (b) of Section 92.201 is liable to a tenant according to this subchapter if:

(1) the information becomes incorrect because a name or address changes; and

(2) the landlord fails to correct the information on or before the seventh day after the date the tenant gives the landlord written notice that the tenant may exercise the remedies under this subchapter if the corrected information is not provided within seven days.

Sec. 92.204. Bad Faith Violation.

A landlord acts in bad faith and is liable according to this subchapter if the landlord gives an incorrect name or address under Subsection (a) of Section 92.201 by wilfully:

(1) disclosing incorrect information under Section 92.201(b)(1) or (2) or Section 92.201(d); or

(2) failing to correct information given under Section 92.201(b)(1) or (2) or Section 92.201(d) that the landlord knows is incorrect.

Sec. 92.205. Remedies.

(a) A tenant of a landlord who is liable under Section 92.202, 92.203, or 92.204 may obtain or exercise one or more of the following remedies:

(1) a court order directing the landlord to make a disclosure required by this subchapter;

(2) a judgment against the landlord for an amount equal to the tenant's actual costs in discovering the information required to be disclosed by this subchapter;

(3) a judgment against the landlord for one month's rent plus $100;

(4) a judgment against the landlord for court costs and attorney's fees; and

(5) unilateral termination of the lease without a court proceeding.

(b) A governmental body whose official or employee has requested information from a landlord who is liable under Section 92.202 or 92.204 may obtain or exercise one or more of the following remedies:

(1) a court order directing the landlord to make a disclosure required by this subchapter;

(2) a judgment against the landlord for an amount equal to the governmental body's actual costs in discovering the information required to be disclosed by this subchapter;

(3) a judgment against the landlord for $500; and

(4) a judgment against the landlord for court costs and attorney's fees.

Sec. 92.206. Landlord's Defense.

A landlord has a defense to liability under Section 92.202 or 92.203 if the tenant owes rent on the date the tenant gives a notice required by either of those sections. Rent delinquency is not a defense for a violation of Section 92.204.

Sec. 92.207. Agents for Delivery of Notice.

(a) A managing or leasing agent, whether residing or maintaining an office on-site or off-site, is the agent of the landlord for purposes of:

(1) notice and other communications required or permitted by this subchapter;

(2) notice and other communications from a governmental body relating to a violation of health, sanitation, safety, or nuisance laws on the landlord's property where the dwelling is located, including notices of:

(A) demands for abatement of nuisances;

(B) repair of a substandard dwelling;

(C) remedy of dangerous conditions;

(D) reimbursement of costs incurred by the governmental body in curing the violation;

(E) fines; and

(F) service of process.

(b) If the landlord's name and business street address in this state have not been furnished in writing to the tenant or government official or employee, the person who collects the rent from a tenant is the landlord's authorized agent for purposes of Subsection (a).

Sec. 92.208. Additional Enforcement by Local Ordinance.

The duties of a landlord and the remedies of a tenant under this subchapter are in lieu of the common law, other statutory law, and local ordinances relating to the disclosure of ownership and management of a dwelling by a landlord to a tenant. However, this subchapter does not prohibit the adoption of a local ordinance that conforms to this subchapter but which contains additional enforcement provisions.

SUBCHAPTER F. SMOKE DETECTORS

Sec. 92.251. Definition.

In this subchapter, "dwelling unit" means a home, mobile home, duplex unit, apartment unit, condominium unit, or any dwelling unit in a multiunit residential structure. It also means a "dwelling" as defined by Section 92.001.

Sec. 92.252. Application of Other Law; Municipal Regulation.

(a) The duties of a landlord and the remedies of a tenant under this subchapter are in lieu of common law, other statutory law, and local ordinances regarding a residential landlord's duty to install, inspect, or repair a smoke detector in a dwelling unit. However, this subchapter does not:

(1) affect a local ordinance adopted before September 1, 1981, that requires landlords to install smoke detectors in new or remodeled dwelling units before September 1, 1981, if the ordinance conforms with or is amended to conform with this subchapter;

(2) limit or prevent adoption or enforcement of a local ordinance relating to fire safety as a part of a building, fire, or housing code, including any requirements relating to the installation of smoke detectors or the type of smoke detectors;

(3) otherwise limit or prevent the adoption of a local ordinance that conforms to this subchapter but which contains additional enforcement provisions, except as provided by Subsection (b); or

(4) affect a local ordinance that requires regular inspections by local officials of smoke detectors in dwelling units and that requires smoke detectors to be operational at the time of inspection.

(b) If a smoke detector powered by battery has been installed in a dwelling unit built before September 1, 1987, in compliance with this subchapter and local ordinances, a local ordinance may not require that a smoke detector powered by alternating current be installed in the unit unless:

(1) the interior of the unit is repaired, remodeled, or rebuilt at a projected cost of more than $2,500 and the repair, remodeling, or rebuilding requires a municipal building permit;

(2) an addition occurs to the unit at a projected cost of more than $2,500;

(3) a smoke detector powered by alternating current was actually installed in the unit at any time prior to September 1, 1987; or

(4) a smoke detector powered by alternating current was required by lawful city ordinance at the time of initial construction of the unit.

Sec. 92.253. Exemptions.

(a) This subchapter does not apply to:

(1) a dwelling unit that is occupied by its owner, no part of which is leased to a tenant;

(2) a dwelling unit in a building five or more stories in height in which smoke detectors are required or regulated by local ordinance; or

(3) a nursing or convalescent home licensed by the Texas Department of Health and certified to meet the Life Safety Code under federal law and regulations.

(b) Notwithstanding this subchapter, a person licensed by the State Board of Insurance to install fire alarms or fire detection devices under Article 5.43-2, Insurance Code, shall comply with that article when installing smoke detectors.

Sec. 92.254. Smoke Detector.

(a) A smoke detector must be:

(1) designed to detect both the visible and invisible products of combustion;

(2) designed with an alarm audible to the bedrooms it serves;

(3) powered by battery, alternating current, or other power source as required by local ordinance;

(4) tested and listed for use as a smoke detector by Underwriters Laboratories, Inc., Factory Mutual Research Corporation, or United States Testing Company, Inc.; and

(5) in good working order.

(b) The power system and installation procedure of a security device that is electrically operated rather than battery operated must comply with applicable local ordinances.

Sec. 92.255. Installation and Location in New Construction.

(a) Before the first tenant takes possession of a dwelling unit, the landlord shall install at least one smoke detector outside, but in the vicinity of, each separate bedroom in the dwelling unit, except:

(1) if the dwelling unit is designed to use a single room for dining, living, and sleeping, the smoke detector must be located inside the room;

(2) if the bedrooms are served by the same corridor, at least one smoke detector must be installed in the corridor in the immediate vicinity of the bedrooms; and

(3) if at least one bedroom is located on a level above the living and cooking area, the smoke detector for the bedrooms must be placed in the center of the ceiling directly above the top of the stairway.

(b) In this section, "bedroom" means a room designed with the intent that it be used for sleeping purposes.

Sec. 92.256. Installation in Units Constructed or Occupied on or Before September 1, 1981.

(a) If the dwelling unit was occupied as a residence on or before September 1, 1981, or the building permit for the unit was issued on or before that date, the landlord shall install at least one smoke detector in accordance with Sections 92.255 and 92.257 on or before September 1, 1984.

(b) Before September 1, 1984, a tenant may install a battery-operated smoke detector in the tenant's dwelling unit without the landlord's prior consent if the installation is made according to Sections 92.255 and 92.257. When the tenant's lease terminates, including after a renewal or extension, the tenant may remove the smoke detector, but the tenant is liable to the landlord for any unnecessary damages to the dwelling unit caused by the removal.

Sec. 92.257. Installation Procedure.

(a) Subject to Subsections (b) and (c), a smoke detector must be installed according to the manufacturer's recommended procedures.

(b) A smoke detector must be installed on a ceiling or wall. If on a ceiling, it must be no closer than six inches to a wall. If on a wall, it must be no closer than six inches and no farther than 12 inches from the ceiling.

(c) A smoke detector may be located other than as required by Subsection (b) if a local ordinance or a local or state fire marshal approves.

Sec. 92.258. Inspection and Repair.

(a) The landlord shall inspect and repair a smoke detector according to this section.

(b) The landlord shall determine that the smoke detector is in good working order at the beginning of the tenant's possession by testing the smoke detector with smoke, by operating the testing button on the smoke detector, or by following other recommended test procedures of the manufacturer for the particular model.

(c) During the term of a lease or during a renewal or extension, the landlord has a duty to inspect and repair a smoke detector, but only if the tenant gives the landlord notice of a malfunction or requests to the landlord that the smoke detector be inspected or repaired. This duty does not exist with respect to damage or a malfunction caused by the tenant, the tenant's family, or the tenant's guests or invitees during the term of the lease or a renewal or extension, except that the landlord has a duty to repair or replace the smoke detector if the tenant pays in advance the reasonable repair or replacement cost, including labor, materials, taxes, and overhead.

(d) The landlord must comply with the tenant's request for inspection or repair within a reasonable time, considering the availability of material, labor, and utilities.

(e) The landlord has met the duty to inspect and repair if the smoke detector is in good working order after the landlord tests the smoke detector with smoke, operates the testing button on the smoke detector, or follows other recommended test procedures of the manufacturer for the particular model.

(f) The landlord is not obligated to provide batteries for a battery-operated smoke detector after a tenant takes possession if the smoke detector was in good working order at the time the tenant took possession.

(g) A smoke detector that is in good working order at the beginning of a tenant's possession is presumed to be in good working order until the tenant requests repair of the smoke detector as provided by this subchapter.

Sec. 92.259. Landlord's Failure to Install, Inspect, or Repair.

(a) A landlord is liable according to this subchapter if:

(1) the landlord did not install a smoke detector at the time of initial occupancy by the tenant as required by this subchapter or a municipal ordinance permitted by this subchapter; or

(2) the landlord does not install, inspect, or repair the smoke detector on or before the seventh day after the date the tenant gives the landlord written notice that the tenant may exercise his remedies under this subchapter if the landlord does not comply with the request within seven days.

(b) If the tenant gives notice under Subsection (a)(2) and the tenant's lease is in writing, the lease may require the tenant to make the initial request for installation, inspection, or repair in writing.

Sec. 92.260. Tenant Remedies.

A tenant of a landlord who is liable under Section 92.259 may obtain or exercise one or more of the following remedies:

(1) a court order directing the landlord to comply with the tenant's request if the tenant is in possession of the dwelling unit;

(2) a judgment against the landlord for damages suffered by the tenant because of the landlord's violation;

(3) a judgment against the landlord for a civil penalty of one month's rent plus $100 if the landlord violates Section 92.259(a)(2);

(4) a judgment against the landlord for court costs;

(5) a judgment against the landlord for attorney's fees in an action under Subdivision (1) or (3); and

(6) unilateral termination of the lease without a court proceeding if the landlord violates Section 92.259(a)(2).

Sec. 92.261. Landlord's Defenses.

The landlord has a defense to liability under Section 92.259 if:

(1) on the date the tenant gives the notice required by, Section 92.259 the tenant has not paid all rent due from the tenant; or

(2) on the date the tenant terminates the lease or files suit the tenant has not fully paid costs requested by the landlord and authorized by Section 92.258.

Sec. 92.2611. Tenant's Disabling of a Smoke Detector.

(a) A tenant is liable according to this subchapter if the tenant removes a battery from a smoke detector without immediately replacing it with a working battery or knowingly disconnects or intentionally damages a smoke detector, causing it to malfunction.

(b) Except as provided in Subsection (c), a landlord of a tenant who is liable under Subsection (a) may obtain a judgment against the tenant for damages suffered by the landlord because the tenant removed a battery from a smoke detector without immediately replacing it with a working battery or knowingly disconnected or intentionally damaged the smoke detector, causing it to malfunction.

(c) A tenant is not liable for damages suffered by the landlord if the damage is caused by the landlord's failure to repair the smoke detector within a reasonable time after the tenant requests it to be repaired, considering the availability of material, labor, and utilities.

(d) A landlord of a tenant who is liable under Subsection (a) may obtain or exercise one or more of the remedies in Subsection (e) if:

(1) a lease between the landlord and tenant contains a notice, in underlined or boldfaced print, which states in substance that the tenant must not disconnect or intentionally damage a smoke detector or remove the battery without immediately replacing it with a working battery and that the tenant may be subject to damages, civil penalties, and attorney's fees under Section 92.2611 of the Property Code for not complying with the notice; and

(2) the landlord has given notice to the tenant that the landlord intends to exercise the landlord's remedies under this subchapter if the tenant does not reconnect, repair, or replace the smoke detector or replace the removed battery within seven days after being notified by the landlord to do so.

The notice in Subdivision (2) must be in a separate document furnished to the tenant after the landlord has discovered that the tenant has disconnected or damaged the smoke detector or removed a battery from it.

(e) If a tenant is liable under Subsection (a) and the tenant does not comply with the landlord's notice under Subsection (d), the landlord shall have the following remedies against the tenant:

(1) a court order directing the tenant to comply with the landlord's notice;

(2) a judgment against the tenant for a civil penalty of one month's rent plus $100;

(3) a judgment against the tenant for court costs; and

(4) a judgment against the tenant for reasonable attorney's fees.

(f) A tenant's guest or invitee who suffers damage because of a landlord's failure to install, inspect, or repair a smoke detector as required by this subchapter may recover a judgment against the landlord for the damage. A tenant's guest or invitee who suffers damage because the tenant removed a battery without immediately replacing it with a working battery or because the tenant knowingly disconnected or intentionally damaged the smoke detector, causing it to malfunction, may recover a judgment against the tenant for the damage.

Sec. 92.262. Agents for Delivery of Notice.

A managing or leasing agent, whether residing or maintaining an office on-site or off-site, is the agent of the landlord for purposes of notice and other communications required or permitted by this subchapter.

SUBCHAPTER G. UTILITY CUTOFF

Sec. 92.301. Landlord Liability to Tenant for Utility Cutoff.

(a) A landlord who has expressly or impliedly agreed in the lease to furnish and pay for water, gas, or electric service to the tenant's dwelling is liable to the tenant if the utility company has cut off utility service to the tenant's dwelling or has given written notice to the tenant that such utility service is about to be cut off because of the landlord's nonpayment of the utility bill.

(b) If a landlord is liable to the tenant under Subsection (a) of this section, the tenant may:

(1) pay the utility company money to reconnect or avert the cutoff of utilities according to this section;

(2) terminate the lease if the termination notice is in writing and move-out is to be within 30 days from the date the tenant has notice from the utility company of a future cutoff or notice of an actual cutoff, whichever is sooner;

(3) deduct from the tenant's rent, without necessity of judicial action, the amounts paid to the utility company to reconnect or avert a cutoff;

(4) if the lease is terminated by the tenant, deduct the tenant's security deposit from the tenant's rent without necessity of lawsuit or obtain a refund of the tenant's security deposit pursuant to law;

(5) if the lease is terminated by the tenant, recover a pro rata refund of any advance rentals paid from the date of termination or the date the tenant moves out, whichever is later;

(6) recover actual damages, including but not limited to moving costs, utility connection fees, storage fees, and lost wages from work; and

(7) recover court costs and attorney's fees, excluding any attorney's fees for a cause of action for damages relating to a personal injury.

(c) When deducting for the tenant's payment of the landlord's utility bill under this section, the tenant shall submit to the landlord a copy of a receipt from the utility company which evidences the amount of payment made by the tenant to reconnect or avert cutoff of utilities.

(d) The tenant remedies under this section are effective on the date the tenant has notice from the utility company of a future cutoff or notice of an actual cutoff, whichever is sooner. However, the tenant's remedies under this section shall cease if:

(1) the landlord provides the tenant with written evidence from the utility that all delinquent sums due the utility have been paid in full; and

(2) at the time the tenant receives such evidence, the tenant has not yet terminated the lease or filed suit under this section.

SUBCHAPTER H. RETALIATION

Sec. 92.331. Retaliation by Landlord.

(a) A landlord may not retaliate against a tenant by taking an action described by Subsection (b) because the tenant:

(1) in good faith exercises or attempts to exercise against a landlord a right or remedy granted to the tenant by lease, municipal ordinance, or federal or state statute;

(2) gives a landlord a notice to repair or exercise a remedy under this chapter; or

(3) complains to a governmental entity responsible for enforcing building or housing codes, a public utility, or a civic or nonprofit agency, and the tenant:

(A) claims a building or housing code violation or utility problem; and

(B) believes in good faith that the complaint is valid and that the violation or problem occurred.

(b) A landlord may not, within six months after the date of the tenant's action under Subsection (a), retaliate against the tenant by:

(1) filing an eviction proceeding, except for the grounds stated by Section 92.332;

(2) depriving the tenant of the use of the premises, except for reasons authorized by law;

(3) decreasing services to the tenant;

(4) increasing the tenant's rent or terminating the tenant's lease; or

(5) engaging, in bad faith, in a course of conduct that materially interferes with the tenant's rights under the tenant's lease.

Sec. 92.332. Nonretaliation.

(a) The landlord is not liable for retaliation under this subchapter if the landlord proves that the action was not made for purposes of retaliation, nor is the landlord liable, unless the action violates a prior court order under Section 92.0563, for:

(1) increasing rent under an escalation clause in a written lease for utilities, taxes, or insurance; or

(2) increasing rent or reducing services as part of a pattern of rent increases or service reductions for an entire multidwelling project.

(b) An eviction or lease termination based on the following circumstances, which are valid grounds for eviction or lease termination in any event, does not constitute retaliation:

(1) the tenant is delinquent in rent when the landlord gives notice to vacate or files an eviction action;

(2) the tenant, a member of the tenant's family, or a guest or invitee of the tenant intentionally damages property on the premises or by word or conduct threatens the personal safety of the landlord, the landlord's employees, or another tenant;

(3) the tenant has materially breached the lease, other than by holding over, by an action such as violating written lease provisions prohibiting serious misconduct or criminal acts, except as provided by this section;

(4) the tenant holds over after giving notice of termination or intent to vacate;

(5) the tenant holds over after the landlord gives notice of termination at the end of the rental term and the tenant does not take action under Section 92.331 until after the landlord gives notice of termination; or

(6) the tenant holds over and the landlord's notice of termination is motivated by a good faith belief that the tenant, a member of the tenant's family, or a guest or invitee of the tenant might:

(A) adversely affect the quiet enjoyment by other tenants or neighbors;

(B) materially affect the health or safety of the landlord, other tenants, or neighbors; or

(C) damage the property of the landlord, other tenants, or neighbors.

Civil Rules of Procedure
Section 1, Rules 737 - 749

Part VII. Rules Relating to Special Proceedings

Section 1. Bill of Discovery

Rule 737. Bill of Discovery

All trial courts shall entertain suits in the nature of bills of discovery, and grant relief therein in accordance with the usages of courts of equity. Such remedy shall be cumulative of all other remedies. In actions of such nature, the plaintiff shall have the right to have the defendant examined on oral interrogatories, either by summoning him to appear for examination before the trial court as in ordinary trials, or by taking his oral deposition in accordance with the general rules relating thereto.

Section 2. Forcible Entry and Detainer

Rule 738. May Sue for Rent.

A suit for rent may be joined with an action of forcible entry and detainer, wherever the suit for rent is within the jurisdiction of the justice court. In such case the court in rendering judgment in the action of forcible entry and detainer, may at the same time render judgment for any rent due the landlord by the renter; provided the amount thereof is within the jurisdiction of the justice court.

Rule 739. Citation

When the party aggrieved or his authorized agent shall file his written sworn complaint with such justice, the justice shall immediately issue citation directed to the defendant or defendants commanding him to appear before such justice at a time and place named in such citation, such time being not more than ten days nor less than six days from the date of service of the citation. The citation shall inform the parties that, upon timely request and payment of a jury fee no later than five days after the defendant is served with citation, the case shall be heard by a jury.

Rule 740. Complainant May Have Possession

The party aggrieved may, at the time of filing his complaint, or thereafter prior to final judgment in the justice court, execute and file a possession bond to be approved by the justice in such amount as the justice may fix as the probable amount of costs of

suit and damages which may result to defendant in the event that the suit has been improperly instituted, and conditioned that the plaintiff will pay defendant all such costs and damages as shall be adjudged against plaintiff. The defendant shall be notified by the justice court that plaintiff has filed a possession bond. Such notice shall be served in the same manner as service of citation and shall inform the defendant of all of the following rules and procedures:

(a) Defendant may remain in possession if defendant executes and files a counterbond prior to the expiration of six days frown the date defendant is served with notice of the filing of plaintiffs bond. Said counterbond shall be approved by the justice and shall be in such amount as the justice may fix as the probable amount of costs of suit and damages which may result to plaintiff in the event possession has been improperly withheld by defendant;

(b) Defendant is entitled to demand and he shall be granted a trial to be held prior to the expiration of six days from the date defendant is served with notice of the filing of plaintiff's possession bond;

(c) If defendant does not file a counterbond and if defendant does not demand that trial be held prior to the expiration of said six-day period, the constable of the precinct or the sheriff of the county where the property is situated, shall place the plaintiff in possession of the property promptly after the expiration of six days from the date defendant is served with notice of the filing of plaintiff's possession bond; and

(d) If, in lieu of a counterbond, defendant demands trial within said six-day period, and if the justice of the peace rules after trial that plaintiff is entitled to possession of the property, the constable or sheriff shall place the plaintiff in possession of the property five days after such determination by the justice of the peace.

Rule 741. Requisites of Complaint

The complaint shall describe the lands, tenements or premises, the possession of which is claimed, with sufficient certainty to identify the same, and it shall also state the facts which entitled the complainant to the possession and authorize the action under Sections 24.001-24.004, Texas Property Code.

Rule 742. Service of Citation

The officer receiving such citation shall execute the same by delivering a copy of it to the defendant, or by leaving a copy thereof with some person over the age of sixteen years, at his usual place of abode, at least six days before the return day thereof; and on or before the day assigned for trial he shall return such citation, with his action written thereon, to the justice who issued the same.

Rule 742a. Service by Delivery to Premises

If the sworn complaint lists all home and work addresses of the defendant which are known to the person filing the sworn complaint and if it states that such person knows of no other home or work addresses of the defendant in the county where the premises are located, service of citation may be by delivery to the premises in question as follows:

If the officer receiving such citation is unsuccessful in serving such citation under Rule 742, the officer shall no later than five days after receiving such citation execute a sworn statement that the officer has made diligent efforts to serve such citation on at least two occasions at all addresses of the defendant in the county where the premises are located as may be shown on the sworn complaint, stating the times and places of attempted service. Such sworn statement shall be filed by the officer with the justice who shall promptly consider the sworn statement of the officer. The justice may then authorize service according to the following:

(a) The officer shall place the citation inside the premises by placing it through a door mail chute or by slipping it under the front door; and if neither method is possible or practical, the officer shall securely affix the citation to the front door or main entry to the premises.

(b) The officer shall that same day or the next day deposit in the mail a true copy of such citation with a copy of the sworn complaint attached thereto, addressed to defendant at the premises in question and sent by first class mail;

(c) The officer shall note on the return of such citation the date of delivery under (a) above and the date of mailing under (b) above; and

(d) Such delivery and mailing to the premises shall occur at least six days before the return day of the citation; and on or before the day assigned for trial he shall return such citation with his action written thereon, to the justice who issued the same.

It shall not be necessary for the aggrieved party or his authorized agent to make request for or motion for alternative service pursuant to this rule.

Rule 743. Docketed

The cause shall be docketed and tried as other cases. If the defendant shall fail to enter an appearance upon the docket in the justice court or file answer before the case is called for trial, the allegations of the complaint may be taken as admitted and judgment by default entered accordingly. The justice shall have authority to issue subpoenas for witnesses to enforce their attendance, and to punish for contempt.

Rule 744. Demanding Jury

Any party shall have the right of trial by jury, by making a request to the court on or before five days from the date the defendant is served with citation, and by paying a jury fee of five dollars. upon such request, a jury shall be summoned as in other cases in justice court.

Rule 745. Trial Postponed

For good cause shown, supported by affidavit of either party, the trial may be postponed not exceeding six days.

Rule 746. Only Issue

In case of forcible entry or of forcible detainer under Sections 24.001-24.008, Texas Property Code, the only issue shall be as to the right to actual possession; and the merits of the title shall not be adjudicated.

Rule 747. Trial

If no jury is demanded by either party, the justice shall try the ease. If a jury is demanded by either party, the jury shall be empaneled and sworn as in other cases; and after hearing the evidence it shall return its verdict in favor of the plaintiff or the defendant as it shall find.

Rule 747a. Representation by Agents

In forcible entry and detainer cases for non-payment of rent or holding, over beyond the rental term, the parties may represent themselves or be represented by their authorized agents in justice court.

Rule 748. Judgment and Writ

If the judgment or verdict be in favor of the plaintiff, the justice shall give judgment for plaintiff for possession of the premises, costs, and damages; and he shall award his writ of possession. If the judgment or verdict be in favor of the defendant, the justice shall give judgment for defendant against the plaintiff for costs and any damages. No writ of possession shall issue until the expiration of five days from the time the judgment is signed.

Rule 749. May Appeal

In appeals in forcible entry and detainer eases, no motion for new trial shall be filed. Either party may appeal from a final judgment in such case, to the county court of the county in which the judgment is rendered by filing with the justice within five days after the judgment is signed, a bond to be approved by said justice, and payable to the adverse party, conditioned that he will prosecute his appeal with effect, or pay all costs and damages which may be adjudged against him. The justice shall set the amount of the bond to include the items enumerated in Rule 162. Within five days following the filing of such bond, the party appealing shall give notice as provided in Rule 21a of the filing of. such bond to the adverse party. No judgment shall be taken by default against the adverse party in the court to which the cause has been appealed without first showing substantial compliance with this rule.

Appendix B
Eviction Flowcharts and Legal Holidays

On the next two pages are flowcharts which show each step in the eviction process. The first one is for an eviction for nonpayment of rent. The second one is for evictions based on the tenant's breach of some clause of the lease other than payment of rent, or for the tenant's violation of some aspect of the Landlord Tenant Act.

Eviction Flow Chart
Eviction with Possession Bond Posted

Start here:

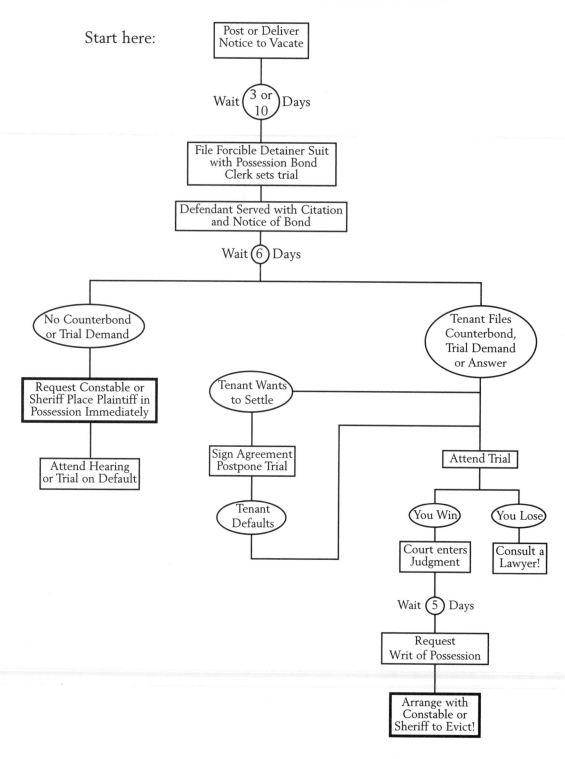

Eviction Flow Chart
Eviction Without Possession Bond Posted

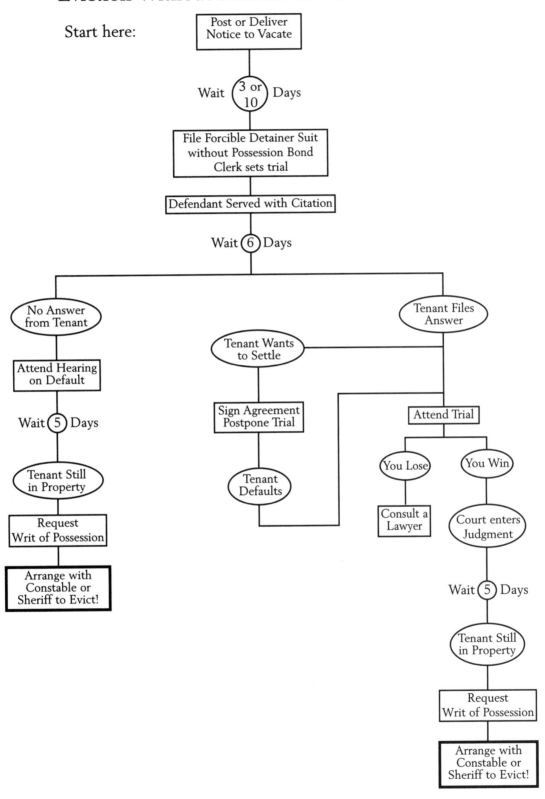

Legal Holidays in Texas

Every Sunday	
New Year's Day	Jan. 1
Martin Luther King, Jr.'s Birthday	Jan. 17
Robert E. Lee's Birthday	Jan. 19
Abraham Lincoln's Birthday	Feb. 12
Susan B. Anthony's Birthday	Feb. 15
George Washington's Birthday	Third Mon. in Feb.
Good Friday	(varies)
Confederate Memorial Day	April 26
Memorial Day	Last Mon. in May
Jefferson Davis' Birthday	June 3
Flag Day	June 14
Independence Day	July 4
Labor Day	First Mon. In Sept.
Columbus Day and Farmers' Day	Second Mon. in Oct.
Veterans' Day	Nov. 11
General Election Day	(varies)
Thanksgiving Day	Fourth Thurs. in Nov.
Christmas Day	Dec. 25

Shrove Tuesday (in counties where carnival associations are organized to celebrate Mardi Gras)

The chief judge of any circuit may designate Rosh Hashanah, Yom Kippur, and Good Friday as legal holidays for the courts within the circuit.

NOTE: When a legal holiday falls on a Sunday, the next day is considered a legal holiday.

Appendix C
Forms

Use of the following forms is described in the text or should be self-explanatory. If you do not understand any aspect of a form, you should seek advice from an attorney.

LICENSE: Although this book is copyrighted, purchasers of the book are granted a license to copy the forms created by the author for their own personal use or use in their law practice.

TABLE OF FORMS

TENANT APPLICATION

Name_____ Date of Birth _____

Name_____ Date of Birth _____

Soc. Sec. Nos. _____

Drivers' License Nos. _____

Children & Ages _____

Present Landlord_____ Phone_____

Address _____ How Long? _____

Previous Landlord_____ Phone_____

Address _____

Second Previous Landlord_____ Phone_____

Address _____

Nearest Relative_____ Phone _____

Address _____

Employer_____ Phone_____

Address _____

Second Applicant's Employer_____Phone _____

Address _____

Pets _____

Other persons who will stay at premises for more than one week_____

_____

Bank Name_____Acct. #_____

Bank Name_____Acct. #_____

Have you ever been evicted?_____

Have you ever been in litigation with a landlord?_____

The undersigned applicants hereby authorize landlord or landlord's representative to obtain and/or verify credit, employment, and rental information.

The undersigned hereby attest that the above information is true.

_____

_____

INSPECTION REPORT

Date: _____

Unit: _____

AREA	CONDITION			
	Move-In		Move-out	
	Good	Poor	Good	Poor
Yard/garden				
Driveway				
Patio/porch				
Exterior				
Entry light/bell				
Living room/Dining room/Halls:				
Floors/carpets				
Walls/ceiling				
Doors/locks				
Fixtures/lights				
Outlets/switches				
Other				
Bedrooms:				
Floors/carpets				
Walls/ceiling				
Doors/locks				
Fixtures/lights				
Outlets/switches				
Other				
Bathrooms:				
Faucets				
Toilet				
Sink/tub				
Floors/carpet				
Walls/ceiling				
Doors/locks				
Fixtures/lights				
Outlets/switches				
Other				
Kitchen:				
Refrigerator				
Range				
Oven				
Dishwasher				
Sink/disposal				
Cabinets/counters				
Floors/carpets				
Walls/ceiling				
Doors/locks				
Fixtures/lights				
Outlets/switches				
Other				
Misc.				
Closets/pantry				
Garage				
Keys				
Other				

PET AGREEMENT

THIS AGREEMENT is made pursuant to that certain Lease dated _____ between _____ as Landlord and _____as Tenant.

In consideration of $_____ as non-refundable cleaning payment and $_____ as additional security deposit paid by Tenant to Landlord, Tenant is allowed to keep the following pet(s): _____ on the premises _____ under the following conditions:

1. In the event the pet produces a litter, Tenant may keep them at the premises no longer than one month past weaning.

2. Tenant shall not engage in any commercial pet-raising activities.

3. No pets other than those listed above shall be kept on the premises without the further written permission of the Landlord.

4. Tenant agrees at all times to keep the pet from becoming a nuisance to neighbors and/or other tenants. This includes controlling the barking of the pet, if necessary and cleaning any animal waste on and about the premises.

5. In the event the pet causes destruction of the property, becomes a nuisance, or Tenant otherwise violates this agreement, Landlord may terminate the Lease according to Texas law.

Date: _____

Landlord: Tenant:

_____   _____

_____   _____

HOUSE OR DUPLEX LEASE

LANDLORD:_____   TENANT:_____

_____   _____

LEASED PREMISES:_____

IN CONSIDERATION of the mutual covenants and agreements herein contained, Landlord hereby leases to Tenant and Tenant hereby leases from Landlord the above-described property under the following terms:

1. TERM. This lease shall be for a term of _____ beginning _____, 20___ and ending _____, 20___.

2. RENT. The rent shall be $_____ per _____ and shall be due on or before the _____ day of each _____. In the event the rent is received more than three (3) days late, a late charge of $_____ shall be due. In the event a check bounces or an eviction notice must be posted, Tenant agrees to pay a $15.00 charge.

3. HOLDING OVER. In the event Tenant holds over beyond the end of the lease term with the consent of the Landlord, a month to month tenancy shall be created, and Tenant shall pay additional rent equal to _____% of the rent payment provided above.

4. PAYMENT. Payment must be received by Landlord on or before the due date at the following address: _____ or such place as designated by Landlord in writing. Tenant understands that this may require early mailing. In the event a check bounces, Landlord may require cash or certified funds.

5. DEFAULT. In the event Tenant defaults under any terms of this lease, Landlord may recover possession as provided by Law and seek monetary damages.

6. SECURITY. Landlord acknowledges receipt of the sum of $_____ as the first and last month's rent under this lease, plus $_____ as security deposit. In the event Tenant terminates the lease prior to its expiration date, said amounts are non-refundable as a charge for Landlord's trouble in securing a new tenant, but Landlord reserves the right to seek additional damages if they exceed the above amounts.

7. UTILITIES. Tenant agrees to pay all utility charges on the property except: _____.

8. MAINTENANCE. Tenant has examined the property, acknowledges it to be in good repair and in consideration of the reduced rental rate, Tenant agrees to keep the premises in good repair and to do all minor maintenance promptly (under $_____ excluding labor) and provide extermination service. <u>Tenant shall repair the following regardless of cost, unless caused by Landlord's negligence: waste water stoppage caused by foreign or improper objects in plumbing lines, damage to doors and windows, damage caused by doors or windows being left open. Tenant shall give Landlord written notice of any condition of the premises Tenant believes materially affects Tenant's health or physical safety. Tenant shall pay for all repair or replacement of security devices if damage is caused by Tenant's misuse.</u>

9. LOCKS. If Tenant adds or changes locks on the premises, Landlord shall be given copies of the keys. Landlord shall at all times have keys for access to the premises in case of emergencies.

10. ASSIGNMENT. This lease may not be assigned by Tenant without the written consent of the Landlord.

11. USE. Tenant shall not use the premises for any illegal purpose or any purpose which will increase the rate of insurance and shall not cause a nuisance for Landlord or neighbors. Tenant shall not create any environmental hazards on the premises.

12. LAWN. Tenant agrees to maintain the lawn and shrubbery on the premises at Tenant's expense.

13. LIABILITY. Tenant shall be responsible for insurance on his own property and agrees not to hold Landlord liable for any damages to Tenant's property on the premises.

14. ACCESS. Landlord reserves the right to enter the premises for the purposes of inspection and to show to prospective purchasers.

15. PETS. No pets shall be allowed on the premises, other than support dogs for disabled persons, except: _____ and there shall be a $_____ non-refundable pet deposit.

16. OCCUPANCY. The premises shall not be occupied by more than _____ adults and _____ children.

17. TENANT'S APPLIANCES. Tenant agrees not to use any heaters, fixtures or appliances drawing excessive current without consent of the Landlord.

18. PARKING. Tenant agrees that no parking is allowed on the premises except: _____ _____. No boats, recreation vehicles or disassembled automobiles may be stored on the premises.

19. FURNISHINGS. Any articles provided to Tenant and listed on attached schedule are to be returned in good condition at the termination of this lease.

20. ALTERATIONS AND IMPROVEMENTS. Tenant shall make no alterations to the property without the written consent of the Landlord and any such alterations or improvements shall become the property of the Landlord.

21. ENTIRE AGREEMENT. This lease constitutes the entire agreement between the parties and may not be modified except in writing signed by both parties.

22. HARASSMENT. Tenant shall not do any acts to intentionally harass the Landlord or other tenants.

23. ATTORNEY'S FEES. In the event it becomes necessary to enforce this Agreement through the services of an attorney, Tenant shall be required to pay Landlord's attorney's fees.

24. SEVERABILITY. In the event any section of this Agreement shall be held to be invalid, all remaining provisions shall remain in full force and effect.

25. RECORDING. This lease shall not be recorded in any public records.

26. WAIVER. Any failure by Landlord to exercise any rights under this Agreement shall not constitute a waiver of Landlord's rights.

27. ABANDONMENT. In the event Tenant abandons the property prior to the expiration of the lease, Landlord may relet the premises and hold Tenant liable for any costs, lost rent or damage to the premises. Lessor may dispose of any property abandoned by Tenant and shall not be responsible to Tenant for any such property.

28. SUBORDINATION. Tenant's interest in the premises shall be subordinate to any encumbrances now or hereafter placed on the premises, to any advances made under such encumbrances, and to any extensions or renewals thereof. Tenant agrees to sign any documents indicating such subordination which may be required by lenders.

29. SURRENDER OF PREMISES. At the expiration of the term of this lease, Tenant shall immediately surrender the premises in as good condition as at the start of this lease.

30. SMOKE DETECTORS. Tenant acknowledges that Tenant has inspected and and all smoke detectors, that smoke detectors are installed, and Tenant agrees to inspect and maintain same, including the installation of fresh batteries, and that Landlord has no obligation to inspect or maintain the smoke detectors. Tenant acknowledges that it is unlawful to disconnect or intentionally damage a smoke detector or remove the battery without immediately replacing it with a working battery, and a tenant who does not comply with this notice is subject to damages, civil penalties, and attorney's fees under Section 92.2611 of the Property Code.

31. Contractual Landlord's Lien: Tenant grants to Landlord a contractual lien on all nonexempt property in, on or about the Leased Premises. Landlord may seize and sell such property to satisfy Tenant's obligations under this lease by proceeding in accordance with Sections 54.044 and 54.045 of the Texas Property Code. Landlord is entitled to collect from the proceeds of any sale or from Tenant the cost of packing, removing and storing any property seized under this provision.

32. MISCELLANEOUS PROVISIONS. _____ _____.

WITNESS the hands and seals of the parties hereto as of this _____ day of _____, 20_____.

LANDLORD: TENANT:

_____   _____

_____   _____

APARTMENT LEASE

LANDLORD:_____   TENANT:_____

_____   _____

LEASED PREMISES:_____   UNIT NO. _____

IN CONSIDERATION of the mutual covenants and agreements herein contained, Landlord hereby leases to Tenant and Tenant hereby leases from Landlord the above-described property under the following terms:

1. TERM. This lease shall be for a term of _____ beginning _____, 20____ and ending _____, 20____.

2. RENT. The rent shall be $_____ per _____ and shall be due on or before the _____ day of each _____. In the event the rent is received more than three (3) days late, a late charge of $_____ shall be due. In the event a check bounces or an eviction notice must be posted, Tenant agrees to pay a $15.00 charge.

3. HOLDING OVER. In the event Tenant holds over beyond the end of the lease term with the consent of the Landlord, a month to month tenancy shall be created, and Tenant shall pay additional rent equal to _____% of the rent payment provided above.

4. PAYMENT. Payment must be received by Landlord on or before the due date at the following address: _____ or such place as designated by Landlord in writing. Tenant understands that this may require early mailing. In the event a check bounces, Landlord may require cash or certified funds.

5. DEFAULT. In the event Tenant defaults under any terms of this lease, Landlord may recover possession as provided by Law and seek monetary damages.

6. SECURITY. Landlord acknowledges receipt of the sum of $_____ as the first and last month's rent under this lease, plus $_____ as security deposit. In the event Tenant terminates the lease prior to its expiration date, said amounts are non-refundable as a charge for Landlord's trouble in securing a new tenant, but Landlord reserves the right to seek additional damages if they exceed the above amounts.

7. UTILITIES. Tenant agrees to pay all utility charges on the property except: _____.

8. MAINTENANCE. Tenant has examined the property, acknowledges it to be in good repair and in consideration of the reduced rental rate, Tenant agrees to keep the premises in good repair and to do all minor maintenance promptly (under $_____ excluding labor) and provide extermination service. Tenant shall repair the following regardless of cost, unless caused by Landlord's negligence: waste water stoppage caused by foreign or improper objects in the plumbing lines serving the premises, damage to doors and windows, damage caused by doors or windows being left open. Tenant shall give Landlord written notice of any condition of the premises Tenant believes materially affects Tenant's health or physical safety. Tenant shall pay for all repair or replacement of security devices if damage is caused by Tenant's misuse.

9. LOCKS. If Tenant adds or changes locks on the premises, Landlord shall be given copies of the keys. Landlord shall at all times have keys for access to the premises in case of emergencies.

10. ASSIGNMENT. This lease may not be assigned by Tenant without the written consent of the Landlord.

11. USE. Tenant shall not use the premises for any illegal purpose or any purpose which will increase the rate of insurance and shall not cause a nuisance for Landlord or neighbors. Tenant shall not create any environmental hazards on the premises.

12. CONDOMINIUM. In the event the premises are a condominium unit, Tenant agrees to abide by all rules, regulations and the declaration of condominium. Maintenance and recreation fees are to be paid by _____. This lease is subject to approval by the condominium association and Tenant agrees to pay any fees necessary for such approval.

13. LIABILITY. Tenant shall be responsible for insurance on his own property and agrees not to hold Landlord liable for any damages to Tenant's property on the premises.

14. ACCESS. Landlord reserves the right to enter the premises for the purposes of inspection and to show to prospective purchasers.

15. PETS. No pets shall be allowed on the premises, other than support dogs for disabled persons, except: _____ and there shall be a $_____ non-refundable pet deposit.

16. OCCUPANCY. The premises shall not be occupied by more than _____ adults and _____ children.

17. TENANT'S APPLIANCES. Tenant agrees not to use any heaters, fixtures or appliances drawing excessive current without consent of the Landlord.

18. PARKING. Tenant agrees that no parking is allowed on the premises except: _____ _____. No boats, recreation vehicles or disassembled automobiles may be stored on the premises.

19. FURNISHINGS. Any articles provided to Tenant and listed on attached schedule are to be returned in good condition at the termination of this lease.

20. ALTERATIONS AND IMPROVEMENTS. Tenant shall make no alterations to the property without the written consent of the Landlord and any such alterations or improvements shall become the property of the Landlord.

21. ENTIRE AGREEMENT. This lease constitutes the entire agreement between the parties and may not be modified except in writing signed by both parties.

22. HARASSMENT. Tenant shall not do any acts to intentionally harass the Landlord or other tenants.

23. ATTORNEY'S FEES. In the event it becomes necessary to enforce this Agreement through the services of an attorney, Tenant shall be required to pay Landlord's attorney's fees.

24. SEVERABILITY. In the event any section of this Agreement shall be held to be invalid, all remaining provisions shall remain in full force and effect.

25. RECORDING. This lease shall not be recorded in any public records.

26. WAIVER. Any failure by Landlord to exercise any rights under this Agreement shall not constitute a waiver of Landlord's rights.

27. ABANDONMENT. In the event Tenant abandons the property prior to the expiration of the lease, Landlord may relet the premises and hold Tenant liable for any costs, lost rent or damage to the premises. Lessor may dispose of any property abandoned by Tenant and shall not be responsible to Tenant for any such property.

28. SUBORDINATION. Tenant's interest in the premises shall be subordinate to any encumbrances now or hereafter placed on the premises, to any advances made under such encumbrances, and to any extensions or renewals thereof. Tenant agrees to sign any documents indicating such subordination which may be required by lenders.

29. SURRENDER OF PREMISES. At the expiration of the term of this lease, Tenant shall immediately surrender the premises in as good condition as at the start of this lease.

30. SMOKE DETECTORS. Tenant acknowledges that Tenant has inspected any and all smoke detectors, that smoke detectors are installed, and Tenant agrees to inspect and maintain same, including the installation of fresh batteries, and that Landlord has no obligation to inspect or maintain the smoke detectors. Tenant acknowledges that it is unlawful to disconnect or intentionally damage a smoke detector or remove the battery without immediately replacing it with a working battery, and a tenant who does not comply with this notice is subject to damages, civil penalties, and attorney's fees under Section 92.2611 of the Property Code.

31. Contractual Landlord's Lien: Tenant grants to Landlord a contractual lien on all nonexempt property in, on or about the Leased Premises. Landlord may seize and sell such property to satisfy Tenant's obligations under this lease by proceeding in accordance with Sections 54.044 and 54.045 of the Texas Property Code. Landlord is entitled to collect from the proceeds of any sale or from Tenant the cost of packing, removing and storing any property seized under this provision.

32. MISCELLANEOUS PROVISIONS. _____ _____.

WITNESS the hands and seals of the parties hereto as of this _____ day of _____, 20_____.
LANDLORD: TENANT:

_____   _____

_____   _____

MONTH TO MONTH LEASE

LANDLORD:_____   TENANT:_____

_____   _____

PROPERTY:_____

IN CONSIDERATION of the mutual covenants and agreements herein contained, Landlord hereby leases to Tenant and Tenant hereby leases from Landlord the above-described property under the following terms:

    1. TERM. This lease shall begin on _____, 20____, and shall be a month-to-month tenancy which may be cancelled by either party upon giving one month's notice to the other party.

    2. RENT. The rent shall be $_____ per month and shall be due on or before the _____ day of each month. In the event the rent is received more than three (3) days late, a late charge of $_____ shall be due. In the event a check bounces or an eviction notice must be posted, Tenant agrees to pay a $15.00 charge.

    3. HOLDING OVER. In the event Tenant holds over beyond the end of the lease term with the consent of the Landlord, a month to month tenancy shall be created, and Tenant shall pay additional rent equal to _____% of the rent payment provided above.

    4. PAYMENT. Payment must be received by Landlord on or before the due date at the following address: _____ or such place as designated by Landlord in writing. Tenant understands that this may require early mailing. In the event a check bounces, Landlord may require cash or certified funds.

    5. DEFAULT. In the event Tenant defaults under any terms of this lease, Landlord may recover possession as provided by Law and seek monetary damages.

    6. SECURITY. Landlord acknowledges receipt of the sum of $_____ as the last month's rent under this lease, plus $_____ as security deposit. In the event Tenant terminates the lease prior to its expiration date, said amounts are non-refundable as a charge for Landlord's trouble in securing a new tenant, but Landlord reserves the right to seek additional damages if they exceed the above amounts.

    7. UTILITIES. Tenant agrees to pay all utility charges on the property except: _____.

    8. MAINTENANCE. Tenant has examined the property, acknowledges it to be in good repair and in consideration of the reduced rental rate, Tenant agrees to keep the premises in good repair and to do all minor maintenance promptly (under $_____ excluding labor) and provide extermination service. Tenant shall repair the following regardless of cost, unless caused by Landlord's negligence: waste water stoppage caused by foreign or improper objects in the plumbing lines serving the premises, damage to doors and windows, damage caused by doors or windows being left open. Tenant shall give Landlord written notice of any condition of the premises Tenant believes materially affects Tenant's health or physical safety. Tenant shall pay for all repair or replacement of security devices if damage is caused by Tenant's misuse.

    9. LOCKS. If Tenant adds or changes locks on the premises, Landlord shall be given copies of the keys. Landlord shall at all times have keys for access to the premises in case of emergencies.

    10. ASSIGNMENT. This lease may not be assigned by Tenant without the written consent of the Landlord.

    11. USE. Tenant shall not use the premises for any illegal purpose or any purpose which will increase the rate of insurance and shall not cause a nuisance for Landlord or neighbors. Tenant shall not create any environmental hazards on the premises.

    12. LAWN. Tenant agrees to maintain the lawn and shrubbery on the premises at his expense.

    13. LIABILITY. Tenant shall be responsible for insurance on his own property and agrees not to hold Landlord liable for any damages to Tenant's property on the premises.

    14. ACCESS. Landlord reserves the right to enter the premises for the purposes of inspection and to show to prospective purchasers.

    15. PETS. No pets shall be allowed on the premises, other than support dogs for disabled persons, except: _____ and there shall be a $_____ non-refundable pet deposit.

16. OCCUPANCY. The premises shall not be occupied by more than _____ adults and _____ children.

17. TENANT'S APPLIANCES. Tenant agrees not to use any heaters, fixtures or appliances drawing excessive current without consent of the Landlord.

18. PARKING. Tenant agrees that no parking is allowed on the premises except: _____ _____. No boats, recreation vehicles or disassembled automobiles may be stored on the premises.

19. FURNISHINGS. Any articles provided to Tenant and listed on attached schedule are to be returned in good condition at the termination of this lease.

20. ALTERATIONS AND IMPROVEMENTS. Tenant shall make no alterations to the property without the written consent of the Landlord and any such alterations or improvements shall become the property of the Landlord.

21. ENTIRE AGREEMENT. This lease constitutes the entire agreement between the parties and may not be modified except in writing signed by both parties.

22. HARASSMENT. Tenant shall not do any acts to intentionally harass the Landlord or other tenants.

23. ATTORNEY'S FEES. In the event it becomes necessary to enforce this Agreement through the services of an attorney, Tenant shall be required to pay Landlord's attorney's fees.

24. SEVERABILITY. In the event any section of this Agreement shall be held to be invalid, all remaining provisions shall remain in full force and effect.

25. RECORDING. This lease shall not be recorded in any public records.

26. WAIVER. Any failure by Landlord to exercise any rights under this Agreement shall not constitute a waiver of Landlord's rights.

27. ABANDONMENT. In the event Tenant abandons the property prior to the expiration of the lease, Landlord may relet the premises and hold Tenant liable for any costs, lost rent or damage to the premises. Lessor may dispose of any property abandoned by Tenant and shall not be responsible to Tenant for any such property.

28. SUBORDINATION. Tenant's interest in the premises shall be subordinate to any encumbrances now or hereafter placed on the premises, to any advances made under such encumbrances, and to any extensions or renewals thereof. Tenant agrees to sign any documents indicating such subordination which may be required by lenders.

29. SURRENDER OF PREMISES. At the expiration of the term of this lease, Tenant shall immediately surrender the premises in as good condition as at the start of this lease.

30. SMOKE DETECTORS. Tenant acknowledges that Tenant has inspected any and all smoke detectors, that smoke detectors are installed, and Tenant agrees to inspect and maintain same, including the installation of fresh batteries, and that Landlord has no obligation to inspect or maintain the smoke detectors. Tenant acknowledges that it is unlawful to disconnect or intentionally damage a smoke detector or remove the battery without immediately replacing it with a working battery, and a tenant who does not comply with this notice is subject to damages, civil penalties, and attorney's fees under Section 92.2611 of the Property Code.

31. Contractual Landlord's Lien: Tenant grants to Landlord a contractual lien on all nonexempt property in, on or about the Leased Premises. Landlord may seize and sell such property to satisfy Tenant's obligations under this lease by proceeding in accordance with Sections 54.044 and 54.045 of the Texas Property Code. Landlord is entitled to collect from the proceeds of any sale or from Tenant the cost of packing, removing and storing any property seized under this provision.

32. MISCELLANEOUS PROVISIONS. _____ _____.

WITNESS the hands and seals of the parties hereto as of this _____ day of _____, 20_____.

LANDLORD: TENANT:

_____   _____

_____   _____

INSPECTION REQUEST

Date:

To:

It will be necessary to enter your dwelling unit for the purpose of _____

_____

_____. If possible we would like

access on _____ at ____o'clock ___.M.

In the event this is not convenient, please call to arrange another time.

Sincerely,

_____

Address:

Phone:

STATEMENT FOR REPAIRS

Date:

To:

    It has been necessary to repair damage to the premises which you occupy which was caused by you or your guests. The costs for repairs were as follows:

    This amount is your responsibility under the terms of the lease and Texas law and should be forwarded to us at the address below.

Sincerely,

_____

Address:

Phone:

NOTICE OF CHANGE OF TERMS

Date:

To:

Dear _____

    You are hereby notified that effective _____ the terms of your rental agreement will be changed as follows:

    If you elect to terminate your tenancy prior to that date kindly provide notice of such election.

                    Sincerely,

                    _____

                    Address:

                    Phone:

LETTER - VACATING TENANT

Date:

To:

Dear _____

    This letter is to remind you that your lease will expire on _____.
Please be advised that we do not intend to renew or extend the lease.

    The keys should be delivered to us at the address below on or before the end of the
lease along with your forwarding address. We will inspect the premises for damages, deduct
any amounts necessary for repairs and refund any remaining balance as required by law.

                      Sincerely,

                      _____

                      Address:

                      Phone:

ANNUAL LETTER - CONTINUATION OF TENANCY

Date:

To:

Dear _____

    This letter is to remind you that your lease will expire on _____.
Please advise us within _____ days as to whether you intend to renew your lease. If so, we
will prepare a new lease for your signature(s).

    If you do not intend to renew your lease, the keys should be delivered to us at the
address below on or before the end of the lease along with your forwarding address. We will
inspect the premises for damages, deduct any amounts necessary for repairs and refund any
remaining balance as required by law.

    If we have not heard from you as specified above we will assume that you will be
vacating the premises and will arrange for a new tenant to move in at the end of your term.

                      Sincerely,

                    _____

                    Address:

                    Phone:

NOTICE OF TERMINATION OF AGENT

Date:

To:

    You are hereby advised that _____ is no longer our agent effective _____. On and after this date he or she is no longer authorized to collect rent, accept notices or to make any representations or agreements regarding the property.

    Rent should thereafter be paid to us directly unless you are instructed otherwise by in writing.

    If you have any questions you may contact us at the address or phone number below.

Sincerely,

_____

Address:

Phone:

NOTICE OF APPOINTMENT OF AGENT

Date:

To:

    You are hereby advised that effective _____, our agent for collection of rent and other matters regarding the property will be _____. However, no terms of the written lease may be modified or waived without our written signature(s).

    If you have any questions you may contact us at the address or phone number below.

               Sincerely,

               _____

               Address:

               Phone:

NOTICE OF SECURITY DEPOSIT DEDUCTIONS
WRITTEN DESCRIPTION AND ITEMIZED LIST

Tenant:_____   Lease Date:_____

Address:_____   Leased Premises:_____

     _____   _____

Date of Notice: _____

1.   Unpaid past due rent for period_____   _____

2.   Repair or replacement of Damaged or Missing Items   _____
     (provide detailed list)

3.   Major Cleaning   _____

4.   Painting   _____

5.   Attorney's Fees   _____

Total: _____

Amount of Security Deposit: _____

     Amount Due to Tenant   _____

     Amount Due from Tenant   _____

NOTICE TO VACATE FOR NONPAYMENT OF RENT

Date: _____

Tenant: _____

Premises
Location: _____

Landlord: _____

Date of Lease: _____

Payment Amount: _____

Payment Frequency _____ (month, week, etc.)

Rental Past Due and Owed: _____

Period Past Due: _____

    Notice is hereby given and demand is hereby made that you (Tenant) vacate the above premises within 3 days after delivery of this notice to such location, for nonpayment of rent.

    You agreed in the above referenced lease to make the payments to Landlord described above, in advance. However, you have failed and refused and continue to fail and refuse to pay the agreed rent for the period described, and owe the Landlord the amount of rent described above, plus any other charges due under the lease.

    If you fail to vacate the premises within 3 days after delivery of this notice, the Landlord will file and prosecute a forcible detainer (eviction) suit against you. Also, if you fail to pay all rent due, the Landlord will file and prosecute a suit against you to recover all rent due and any other charges due under the lease.

Landlord:_____

By:_____
Authorized Agent

NOTICE TO VACATE FOR NONPAYMENT OF RENT

Date: _____

Tenant: _____

Premises
Location: _____

Landlord: _____

Date of Lease: _____

Payment Amount: _____

Payment Frequency _____ (month, week, etc.)

Rental Past Due and Owed: _____

Period Past Due: _____

Notice is hereby given and demand is hereby made that you (Tenant) vacate the above premises within 10 days after delivery of this notice to such location, for nonpayment of rent.

You agreed in the above referenced lease to make the payments to Landlord described above, in advance. However, you have failed and refused and continue to fail and refuse to pay the agreed rent for the period described, and owe the Landlord the amount of rent described above, plus any other charges due under the lease.

If you fail to vacate the premises within 10 days after delivery of this notice, the Landlord will file and prosecute a forcible detainer (eviction) suit against you. Also, if you fail to pay all rent due, the Landlord will file and prosecute a suit against you to recover all rent due and any other charges due under the lease.

If you have failed to vacate the premises within such ten day period, and the Landlord files suit against you, judgment may be obtained against you for reasonable attorney's fees plus costs of court, in addition to recovery of rent and other charges due under the lease.

Landlord:_____

By:_____
Authorized Agent

NOTICE TO VACATE FOR BREACH OF LEASE (NON-RENT)

Date: _____

Tenant: _____

Premises Location:

_____

_____

Landlord: _____

Date of Lease: _____

Date of Breach: _____

Lease Paragraph No: _____

Nature of Breach: _____

_____

You agreed in the above referenced lease to perform certain obligations in addition to the payment of rent. However, you have committed a material and substantial breach of the lease as described above. The Landlord is exercising his right under the lease to terminate your right to occupy the premises based on this breach.

Notice is hereby given and demand is hereby made that you (Tenant) vacate the above premises within 3 days after delivery of this notice to such location, for the above described breach of your lease.

If you fail to vacate the premises within 3 days after delivery of this notice, the Landlord will file and prosecute a forcible detainer (eviction) suit against you (eviction suit).

Landlord:_____

By:_____
Authorized Agent

Notice to Vacate for Holding Over

Date: _____

Tenant: _____

Premises Location:

_____

_____

Landlord: _____

Date of Lease: _____

Date Lease Term or Extension Period Ended:

_____

The lease term or extension period under the above referenced lease ended on the date indicated above. You have not vacated the premises and are holding over beyond the end of the lease term or extension period.

Notice is hereby given and demand is hereby made that you (Tenant) vacate the above premises <u>immediately</u>.

If you fail to vacate the premises immediately, you may be subject to a forcible detainer (eviction) suit, change of locks permitted by law, holdover rent under the lease, damages which may be suffered by the Landlord and/or prospective tenants, and attorney's fees. Landlord may also treat your holdover as an extension of your obligations under the lease for an additional month.

If you fail to vacate the premises within 3 days after delivery of this notice, the Landlord will file and prosecute a forcible detainer (eviction) suit against you.

Landlord:_____

By:_____
Authorized Agent

MAIL 5 DAYS IN ADVANCE

HAND DELIVER 3 DAYS IN ADVANCE

ADVANCE NOTICE OF INTENT TO CHANGE LOCKS

Date: _____

Tenant: _____

Premises Location:

_____

_____

Landlord: _____

Date of Lease: _____

Rental Due: _____

      You are delinquent in payment of rent under the above lease. The Landlord intends to change your locks on _____ if your rent is not brought current before such date. Please avoid the embarrassment and difficulty which may result from such procedure by paying the past due rent immediately. You can pay such delinquent rent between _____ A.M. and _____ P.M. (normal business hours) at _____.

Landlord:_____

By:_____
Authorized Agent

NOTICE OF CHANGING LOCKS
FOR NONPAYMENT OF RENT UNDER RESIDENTIAL LEASE

Tenant:_____

Leased Premises: _____

_____

RE: Notice of changing Locks for Nonpayment of Rent

       _____

Dear Tenant:

      Pursuant to Property Code Section 92.0081, I have exercised the Landlord's rights under the above lease to change your door lock because you are delinquent in payment of rent. You may obtain a key from me at any hour by calling _____. A new key will be delivered within two hours of your call. The landlord must provide you a new key regardless of whether or not you pay any delinquent rent.

Amount of delinquent rent: _____

Amount of other delinquent charges: _____

          Landlord:_____

          By:_____

NOTICE CONCERNING WRONGFUL WITHHOLDING OF RENT

Date:_____

Tenant:_____

Premises Location:

_____

_____

Landlord:_____

Date of Lease:_____

Amount of Rent Past Due:_____

Date Rent Due:_____

You have not paid the rent due under the above lease on the date due. I have reason to believe you may be withholding rent for an alleged failure of the landlord to make repairs of remedy a condition of the premises. If you have a complaint regarding the condition of the premises, please contact me at the address and telephone number below. However, if you wrongfully withhold or deduct rent or make repairs not authorized by the lease or the Texas Property Code, the Landlord intends to pursue all available legal remedies, including but not limited to filing a forcible detainer (eviction) suit for nonpayment of rent, and damages under Section 92.058 of the Texas Property Code.

Section 92.058 provides:

Section 92.058. LANDLORD REMEDY FOR TENANT VIOLATION.

(a)   If the tenant withholds rents, causes repairs to be performed, or makes rent deductions for repairs in violation of this subchapter, the landlord may recover actual damages from the tenant. If, after a landlord has notified a tenant in writing of (1) the illegality of the tenant's rent withholding or the tenant's proposed repair and (2) the penalties of this subchapter, the tenant withholds rent, causes repairs to be performed, or make rent deductions for repairs in bad faith violation of this subchapter, the landlord may recover from the tenant a civil penalty of one month's rent plus $500.

(b)   Notice under this section must be in writing and may be given in person, by mail, or by delivery to the premises.

Landlord: _____

By: _____
　　　　　　　Authorized Representative

Printed Name: _____

Address:　　_____

　　　　　　　_____

Telephone:　_____

Notice of Extension of Lease Due to Tenant Holding Over

Date:_____

Tenant:_____

Premises Location:

_____

_____

Landlord:_____

Date of Lease:_____

Date Lease term or Extension Period Ended:

_____

Increased Monthly Rental Amount:_____

Per Diem Rent:_____

You (Tenant) failed to vacate the above premises by the above date when the lease term or extension period ended. Such failure to vacate constitutes an unlawful holding over. Pursuant to the terms of the above lease, if the Landlord consents to such holdover, a month-to month tenancy is created and you are liable for the increased rental provided above, beginning on the above date and ending on the date you vacate the premises.

Notice is hereby given and demand is hereby made that you vacate the premises on _____. If you fail to pay the increased monthly rental within 3 days of this date, you will be subject to a forcible detainer (eviction) suit and other legal remedies available to Landlord.

Landlord:_____

By:_____
Authorized Agent

(NOTE: Use the second paragraph only if you want the tenant to move at the end of the current month. You must give him at least 30 days notice if you consent to his holdover and a month-to-month tenancy is created).

Notice of Exercise of Contractual Lien

Date:_____

Tenant:_____

Premises Location:

_____

_____

Landlord:_____

Date of Lease:_____

Past Due Rent Due:_____

Date Rent Due:_____

     Because you are in default under the above referenced lease for nonpayment of rent, the Landlord has exercised his rights under the contractual lien provision of the lease by entering the above premises and seizing nonexempt property found there. A copy of the itemized list made of such property is attached to this notice. Upon full payment of the delinquent (past due) rent, the property will be promptly returned to you.

     You may contact me at the address and telephone number below regarding the amount owed and to discuss resolving this matter. If you do not pay the past due rent immediately, your property will be sold in accordance with Section 54.045 of the Texas Property Code.

                    Landlord:_____

                    By:_____
                           Authorized Representative
                    Printed Name of Representative:

                    _____

                    Address:_____

                    _____

                    Telephone:_____

This notice, along with the itemized list of property must, by law, be left in a conspicuous place inside the dwelling. A

AGREEMENT TO POSTPONE EVICTION
AND PAYMENT OF PAST DUE RENT

Date: _____

Tenant: _____

Premises Location:

_____

_____

Landlord: _____

Lease Date: _____

Past Due Rent: _____

For Months of: _____

Other Charges: _____

(Late Fees, Eviction Suit Fees. etc.)

Cause No. (If filed): _____

Tenant acknowledges he owes Landlord the above amounts under the above referenced lease, and that Landlord has the right to prosecute a forcible detainer (eviction) suit against Tenant for breach of such lease.

Tenant agrees to pay the amount due under the lease pursuant to the following payment schedule:

Date   Amount

_____   _____

_____   _____

_____   _____

_____   _____

Notwithstanding the above agreement and any of the payments described above, Landlord may, at Landlord's option, begin or continue the eviction process, including but not limited to giving notice to vacate, filing a forcible detainer suit and obtaining service on Tenant. Provided, however, that so long as the above payments are timely made accordingly to the above schedule, and Tenant is current in the payment of all future rent due under the lease during the payment schedule, Landlord shall not seek a default judgment or request a trial on the forcible detainer suit.

If Tenant does not timely make the above payments or does not timely make future rental payments, Landlord will be entitled to submit this agreement to the Justice of the Peace and obtain a judgment for possession of the premises. Tenant agrees to voluntarily move out upon failure to make any agreed payment.

When all past due rents and other amounts due are paid according to the above schedule, Landlord shall dismiss any forcible detainer suit filed.

Date:_____

Landlord:_____

By:_____
Authorized Agent

Date:_____

_____
Tenant

JP DOCKET NO._____

Case No._____

In the Justice Court

Precinct_____Place_____

_____, Texas

Plaintiff:_____

(Landlord's Name)

vs.

Defendants:_____

_____

DEFENDANT'S:

SOCIAL SECURITY #_____

DATE OF BIRTH_____

DRIVER'S LICENSE #_____

SWORN COMPLAINT FOR FORCIBLE DETAINER

❑ With Bond for Possession

❑ With Suit for Rent

1. **COMPLAINT.** Plaintiff (Landlord) hereby complains of the defendants named above for forcible detainer of plaintiff's premises (including storerooms and parking areas) located in the above precinct, to wit.

_____

Street Address   Unit No. (if any)   City   State   Zip

2. **SERVICE OF CITATION.** Service is requested on defendants by personal service at home or work or by alternative service under Rule 742. If necessary, alternative service is requested under Rule 742a Defendant's home addresses are:

_____

Plaintiff knows of no other home or work addresses of defendants in the county where the premises described in paragraph 1 are located.

3. **UNPAID RENT AS GROUNDS FOR EVICTION.** Plaintiff and defendants entered into a rental agreement for the above described premises, for occupancy commencing on the _____day of_____, 20____. Defendants failed to pay the following rental amounts which were demanded by plaintiff and which were due on the following dates (list amount and dates)_____

_____

Total Delinquent Rent This Date$_____   Daily Prorated Amount$_____

4. **HOLDOVER AS GROUNDS FOR EVICTION.** Defendants are unlawfully holding over since they failed to vacate at the end of the rental term or renewal or extension period, which was the _____day of _____, _____.

5. **OTHER GROUNDS FOR EVICTION.** plaintiff's other grounds for eviction of defendants are as follows:

_____

_____

6. **NOTICE TO VACATE.** Plaintiff has given defendants a written notice to vacate and demand for possession. Such notice was delivered to defendants on the _____day of_____,_____, by personal delivery or mail.

7. **FAILURE TO VACATE.** Defendants failed to vacate or comply with plaintiff's written demand for possession of the premises.

8. **BOND FOR POSSESSION.** If plaintiff has filed a "Bond for Possession" under Rule 740, plaintiff requests (1) that the amount of plaintiff's bond and defendants' counterbond be set, (2) that plaintiff's bond be approved by the Court, and (3) that notice as required by Rule 740 be given to defendants regarding counterbond or early trial.

9. **REQUEST FOR JUDGMENT.** Plaintiff prays that defendants be served with citation and that plaintiff have judgment against defendants for: possession of the premises, including removal of defendants and defendants for: possession from the premises; unpaid rent as set forth above; attorney's fees; court costs, and interest on the above sums at the rate stated in the rental contract, or if not so stated, at the_____statutory rate for judgments under Article 5069-10.5

_____

Signature of Plaintiff (landlord) or agent

_____

_____   Address of Plaintiff (landlord) or Agent

Date

City   State   Zip

_____

Telephone No. of plaintiff (Landlord) or agent

Sworn to and subscribed before me this the_____day of_____,_____

_____

CLERK OF THE JUSTICE COURT

NOTARY PUBLIC FOR STATE OF TEXAS

(STRIKE ONE)

NOTICE OF SALE OF SEIZED OR ABANDONED PROPERTY

CERTIFIED MAIL, RETURN RECEIPT REQUESTED
AND REGULAR UNITED STATES MAIL

Date: _____

Tenant (or Former Tenant): _____

Last Known Address: _____

_____

Premises Location: _____

Landlord: _____

Date of Lease: _____

Unpaid Rent Due: _____

for Months of: _____

Packing & Removing Costs: _____

Storage Costs: _____

Storage Per Diem: _____

Date and Time of Sale: _____

Place of Sale: _____

_____

Notice is hereby given you (Tenant or Former Tenant) that the property removed from the above premises will be sold at a public or private sale on the date provided above, at the location described above, to satisfy the amount you owe the Landlord under the above referenced lease.

The property was either seized pursuant to a contractual lien contained in the lease or removed from the premises after you abandoned same upon vacating the premises.

The date of the sale is at least 30 days after the mailing date of this notice.

You have the right to redeem the property at any time before it its sold by paying the Landlord all delinquent rents, and all reasonable packing, removal, storage and sale costs.

You can contact me at the address and telephone number below regarding this sale, the amount owed, and your right to redeem the property.

The property will be sold to the highest cash bidder. It will be sold subject to any recorded chattel mortgage or financing statement. Proceeds shall be applied first to unpaid rent, then to packing, removing, storage and sale costs. Any remaining sale proceeds will be mailed to you at your last known address not later than the 30th day after the date of sale.

Landlord: _____

By: _____
Authorized Representative
Printed Name of Representative: _____

_____

Address: _____

_____

Telephone: _____

Section 54.045 requires this notice be sent regular mail and certified mail, return receipt requested not later than the 30th day before the date of sale.

JP-67   GPC-1084 Rev. 1-88
Court

APPEAL BOND - Civil Justice

_____

_____

     vs.

_____

_____

In Justice Court, Precinct No._____

_____ County, Texas

No._____

WHEREAS, on the _____ day of _____ A.D. 20_____,
before _____ a Justice of the Peace in and for Precinct No. _____
of the County of Tarrant, State of Texas,_____
_____ recovered a judgment
against_____ for the sum
of_____DOLLARS, besides
Costs of suit, from which Judgment the said_____
ha_____ appealed to the County Court at Law No._____of Tarrant County, Texas.

     NOW THEREFORE, we_____
_____, as Principal_____,
and_____
as Sureties, acknowledge ourselves bound to pay unto the said_____
_____ the sum of _____DOLLARS,
conditioned that the said_____
shall prosecute_____said appeal to effect, and shall pay off and satisfy the
judgment which may be rendered against_____on such appeal.

     WITNESS our hands, this_____day of_____ A.D. 20_____.

Approved:

_____
    Justice of the Peace, Precinct No._____
    _____ County, Texas

_____Principal _____.

_____ Surety.

_____ Surety.

_____ Surety.

* Double the amount of the Judgment.

168

AFFIDAVIT AS TO SUFFICIENCY OF SURETY

STATE OF TEXAS

COUNTY OF _____

I _____, do hereby swear that I am worth in my own right at least the sum of $_____ which is the amount in which I am bound by the attached bond after deducting from my property all that which is exempt by the Constitution and laws of the State of Texas from forced sale, and after the payment of all my debts of every description, whether individual or security debts, and after satisfying all incumbrances upon my property which are known to me, and I reside in _____ County, Texas, and have property in this State liable to execution worth $_____ the amount in which I am bound, or more.

_____
Signature

_____
Address

_____
City   Zip Code

(_____)_____
Phone

Sworn to and subscribed before me by the said _____ on this the _____ day of _____, 20_____.

_____
Notary Public, State of Texas

Disclosure of Information on Lead-Based Paint and/or Lead-Based Paint Hazards

Lead Warning Statement
Housing built before 1978 may contain lead-based paint. Lead from paint, paint chips, and dust can pose health hazards if not managed properly. Lead exposure is especially harmful to young children and pregnant women. Before renting pre-1978 housing, lessors must disclose the presence of known lead-based paint and/or lead-based paint hazards in the dwelling. Lessees must also receive a federally approved pamphlet on lead poisoning prevention.

Lessor's Disclosure
(a) Presence of lead-based paint and/or lead-based paint hazards (Check (i) or (ii) below):

(i)_____ Known lead-based paint and/or lead-based paint hazards are present in the housing (explain).

_____

(ii)_____ Lessor has no knowledge of lead-based paint and/or lead-based paint hazards in the housing.

(b) Records and reports available to the lessor (Check (i) or (ii) below):

(i)_____ Lessor has provided the lessee with all available records and reports pertaining to lead-based paint and/or lead-based paint hazards in the housing (list documents below).

_____

(ii)_____ Lessor has no reports or records pertaining to lead-based paint and/or lead-based paint hazards in the housing.

Lessee's Acknowledgment (initial)
(c)_____ Lessee has received copies of all information listed above.
(d)_____ Lessee has received the pamphlet Protect Your Family from Lead in Your Home.

Agent's Acknowledgment (initial)
(e)_____ Agent has informed the lessor of the lessor's obligations under 42 U.S.C. 4852d and is aware of his/her responsibility to ensure compliance.

Certification of Accuracy
The following parties have reviewed the information above and certify, to the best of their knowledge, that the information they have provided is true and accurate.

Lessor	Date	Lessor	Date

Lessee	Date	Lessee	Date

Agent	Date	Agent	Date

Amendment to Lease/Rental Agreement

The undersigned parties to that certain agreement dated _____,
_____ on the premises known as _____,
hereby agree to amend said agreement as follows:

WITNESS the hands and seals of the parties hereto this ____ day of _____,
_____.

Landlord: Tenant:

_____   _____

_____   _____

INDEX

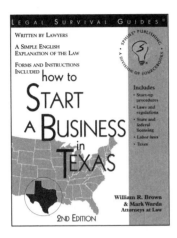
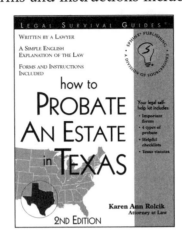
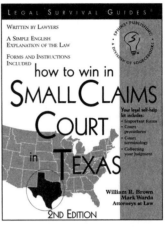

SPHINX® PUBLISHING'S NATIONAL TITLES

Valid in All 50 States

LEGAL SURVIVAL IN BUSINESS

How to Form a Limited Liability Company	$19.95
How to Form Your Own Corporation (2E)	$19.95
How to Form Your Own Partnership	$19.95
How to Register Your Own Copyright (3E)	$19.95
How to Register Your Own Trademark (3E)	$19.95
Most Valuable Business Legal Forms You'll Ever Need (2E)	$19.95
Most Valuable Corporate Forms You'll Ever Need (2E)	$24.95
Software Law (with diskette)	$29.95

LEGAL SURVIVAL IN COURT

Crime Victim's Guide to Justice	$19.95
Debtors' Rights (3E)	$12.95
Defend Yourself against Criminal Charges	$19.95
Grandparents' Rights (2E)	$19.95
Help Your Lawyer Win Your Case (2E)	$12.95
Jurors' Rights (2E)	$9.95
Legal Malpractice and Other Claims against Your Lawyer	$18.95
Legal Research Made Easy (2E)	$14.95
Simple Ways to Protect Yourself from Lawsuits	$24.95
Winning Your Personal Injury Claim	$19.95

LEGAL SURVIVAL IN REAL ESTATE

How to Buy a Condominium or Townhome	$16.95
How to Negotiate Real Estate Contracts (3E)	$16.95
How to Negotiate Real Estate Leases (3E)	$16.95
Successful Real Estate Brokerage Management	$19.95

LEGAL SURVIVAL IN PERSONAL AFFAIRS

Guia de Inmigracion a Estados Unidos (2E)	$19.95
How to File Your Own Bankruptcy (4E)	$19.95
How to File Your Own Divorce (3E)	$19.95
How to Fire Your First Employee	$19.95
How to Hire Your First Employee	$19.95
How to Make Your Own Will (2E)	$12.95
How to Write Your Own Living Will (2E)	$9.95
How to Write Your Own Premarital Agreement (2E)	$19.95
How to Win Your Unemployment Compensation Claim	$19.95
Living Trusts and Simple Ways to Avoid Probate (2E)	$19.95
Neighbor v. Neighbor (2E)	$12.95
The Nanny and Domestic Help Legal Kit	$19.95
The Power of Attorney Handbook (3E)	$19.95
Simple Ways to Protect Yourself from Lawsuits	$24.95
Social Security Benefits Handbook (2E)	$14.95
Unmarried Parents' Rights	$19.95
U.S.A. Immigration Guide (3E)	$19.95
Your Right to Child Custody, Visitation and Support	$19.95

Legal Survival Guides are directly available from Sourcebooks, Inc., or from your local bookstores.

For credit card orders call 1–800–43–BRIGHT, write P.O. Box 4410, Naperville, IL 60567-4410 or fax 630-961-2168

SPHINX® PUBLISHING ORDER FORM

<table>
<tr><td>BILL TO:</td><td>SHIP TO:</td></tr>
</table>

Phone #	Terms	F.O.B. Chicago, IL	Ship Date

Charge my: ☐ VISA ☐ MasterCard ☐ American Express

☐ **Money Order or Personal Check**

Credit Card Number

Expiration Date

Qty	ISBN	Title	Retail	Ext.	Qty	ISBN	Title	Retail	Ext.
		SPHINX PUBLISHING NATIONAL TITLES				1-57071-345-6	Most Valuable Bus. Legal Forms You'll Ever Need (2E)	$19.95	
	1-57071-166-6	Crime Victim's Guide to Justice	$19.95			1-57071-346-4	Most Valuable Corporate Forms You'll Ever Need (2E)	$24.95	
	1-57071-342-1	Debtors' Rights (3E)	$12.95			1-57248-089-0	Neighbor v. Neighbor (2E)	$12.95	
	1-57071-162-3	Defend Yourself against Criminal Charges	$19.95			1-57071-348-0	The Power of Attorney Handbook (3E)	$19.95	
	1-57248-082-3	Grandparents' Rights (2E)	$19.95			1-57248-020-3	Simple Ways to Protect Yourself from Lawsuits	$24.95	
	1-57248-087-4	Guia de Inmigracion a Estados Unidos (2E)	$19.95			1-57071-337-5	Social Security Benefits Handbook (2E)	$14.95	
	1-57248-103-X	Help Your Lawyer Win Your Case (2E)	$12.95			1-57071-163-1	Software Law (w/diskette)	$29.95	
	1-57071-164-X	How to Buy a Condominium or Townhome	$16.95			0-913825-86-7	Successful Real Estate Brokerage Mgmt.	$19.95	
	1-57071-223-9	How to File Your Own Bankruptcy (4E)	$19.95			1-57248-098-X	The Nanny and Domestic Help Legal Kit	$19.95	
	1-57071-224-7	How to File Your Own Divorce (3E)	$19.95			1-57071-399-5	Unmarried Parents' Rights	$19.95	
	1-57248-083-1	How to Form a Limited Liability Company	$19.95			1-57071-354-5	U.S.A. Immigration Guide (3E)	$19.95	
	1-57248-100-5	How to Form a DE Corporation from Any State	$19.95			0-913825-82-4	Victims' Rights	$12.95	
	1-57248-101-3	How to Form a NV Corporation from Any State	$19.95			1-57071-165-8	Winning Your Personal Injury Claim	$19.95	
	1-57248-099-8	How to Form a Nonprofit Corporation	$24.95			1-57248-097-1	Your Right to Child Custody, Visitation and Support	$19.95	
	1-57071-227-1	How to Form Your Own Corporation (2E)	$19.95				**CALIFORNIA TITLES**		
	1-57071-343-X	How to Form Your Own Partnership	$19.95			1-57071-360-X	CA Power of Attorney Handbook	$12.95	
	1-57248-125-0	How to Fire Your First Employee	$19.95			1-57248-126-9	How to File for Divorce in CA (2E)	$19.95	
	1-57248-121-8	How to Hire Your First Employee	$19.95			1-57071-356-1	How to Make a CA Will	$12.95	
	1-57248-119-6	How to Make Your Own Will (2E)	$12.95			1-57071-408-8	How to Probate an Estate in CA	$19.95	
	1-57071-331-6	How to Negotiate Real Estate Contracts (3E)	$16.95			1-57248-116-1	How to Start a Business in CA	$16.95	
	1-57071-332-4	How to Negotiate Real Estate Leases (3E)	$16.95			1-57071-358-8	How to Win in Small Claims Court in CA	$14.95	
	1-57248-124-2	How to Register Your Own Copyright (3E)	$19.95			1-57071-359-6	Landlords' Rights and Duties in CA	$19.95	
	1-57248-104-8	How to Register Your Own Trademark (3E)	$19.95				**FLORIDA TITLES**		
	1-57071-349-9	How to Win Your Unemployment Compensation Claim	$19.95			1-57071-363-4	Florida Power of Attorney Handbook (2E)	$12.95	
	1-57248-118-8	How to Write Your Own Living Will (2E)	$9.95			1-57248-093-9	How to File for Divorce in FL (6E)	$21.95	
	1-57071-344-8	How to Write Your Own Premarital Agreement (2E)	$19.95			1-57248-086-6	How to Form a Limited Liability Co. in FL	$19.95	
	1-57071-333-2	Jurors' Rights (2E)	$9.95			1-57071-401-0	How to Form a Partnership in FL	$19.95	
	1-57248-032-7	Legal Malpractice and Other Claims against...	$18.95			1-57071-380-4	How to Form a Corporation in FL (4E)	$19.95	
	1-57071-400-2	Legal Research Made Easy (2E)	$14.95				*Form Continued on Following Page*	**SUBTOTAL**	
	1-57071-336-7	Living Trusts and Simple Ways to Avoid Probate (2E)	$19.95						

To order, call Sourcebooks at 1-800-43-BRIGHT® or FAX (630)961-2168 (Bookstores, libraries, wholesalers—please call for discount)

SPHINX® PUBLISHING ORDER FORM

Qty	ISBN	Title	Retail	Ext.
		FLORIDA TITLES (CONT'D)		
_____	1-57071-361-8	How to Make a FL Will (5E)	$12.95	_____
_____	1-57248-088-2	How to Modify Your FL Divorce Judgment (4E)	$22.95	_____
_____	1-57071-364-2	How to Probate an Estate in FL (3E)	$24.95	_____
_____	1-57248-081-5	How to Start a Business in FL (5E)	$16.95	_____
_____	1-57071-362-6	How to Win in Small Claims Court in FL (6E)	$14.95	_____
_____	1-57071-335-9	Landlords' Rights and Duties in FL (7E)	$19.95	_____
_____	1-57071-334-0	Land Trusts in FL (5E)	$24.95	_____
_____	0-913825-73-5	Women's Legal Rights in FL	$19.95	_____
		GEORGIA TITLES		
_____	1-57071-376-6	How to File for Divorce in GA (3E)	$19.95	_____
_____	1-57248-075-0	How to Make a GA Will (3E)	$12.95	_____
_____	1-57248-076-9	How to Start a Business in Georgia (3E)	$16.95	_____
		ILLINOIS TITLES		
_____	1-57071-405-3	How to File for Divorce in IL (2E)	$19.95	_____
_____	1-57071-415-0	How to Make an IL Will (2E)	$12.95	_____
_____	1-57071-416-9	How to Start a Business in IL (2E)	$16.95	_____
_____	1-57248-078-5	Landlords' Rights & Duties in IL	$19.95	_____
		MASSACHUSETTS TITLES		
_____	1-57071-329-4	How to File for Divorce in MA (2E)	$19.95	_____
_____	1-57248-115-3	How to Form a Corporation in MA	$19.95	_____
_____	1-57248-108-0	How to Make a MA Will (2E)	$12.95	_____
_____	1-57248-109-9	How to Probate an Estate in MA (2E)	$19.95	_____
_____	1-57248-106-4	How to Start a Business in MA (2E)	$16.95	_____
_____	1-57248-107-2	Landlords' Rights and Duties in MA (2E)	$19.95	_____
		MICHIGAN TITLES		
_____	1-57071-409-6	How to File for Divorce in MI (2E)	$19.95	_____
_____	1-57248-077-7	How to Make a MI Will (2E)	$12.95	_____
_____	1-57071-407-X	How to Start a Business in MI (2E)	$16.95	_____
		MINNESOTA TITLES		
_____	1-57248-039-4	How to File for Divorce in MN	$19.95	_____
_____	1-57248-040-8	How to Form a Simple Corporation in MN	$19.95	_____
_____	1-57248-037-8	How to Make a MN Will	$9.95	_____
_____	1-57248-038-6	How to Start a Business in MN	$16.95	_____
		NEW YORK TITLES		
_____	1-57071-184-4	How to File for Divorce in NY	$19.95	_____
_____	1-57248-105-6	How to Form a Corporation in NY	$19.95	_____
_____	1-57248-095-5	How to Make a NY Will (2E)	$12.95	_____
_____	1-57071-185-2	How to Start a Business in NY	$16.95	_____
_____	1-57071-187-9	How to Win in Small Claims Court in NY	$14.95	_____
_____	1-57071-186-0	Landlords' Rights and Duties in NY	$19.95	_____
_____	1-57071-188-7	New York Power of Attorney Handbook	$19.95	_____
_____	1-57248-122-6	Tenants' Rights in NY	$14.95	_____
		NORTH CAROLINA TITLES		
_____	1-57071-326-X	How to File for Divorce in NC (2E)	$19.95	_____
_____	1-57071-327-8	How to Make a NC Will (2E)	$12.95	_____
_____	1-57248-096-3	How to Start a Business in NC (2E)	$16.95	_____
_____	1-57248-091-2	Landlords' Rights & Duties in NC	$19.95	_____
		OHIO TITLES		
_____	1-57248-102-1	How to File for Divorce in OH	$19.95	_____
		PENNSYLVANIA TITLES		
_____	1-57248-127-7	How to File for Divorce in PA (2E)	$19.95	_____
_____	1-57248-094-7	How to Make a PA Will (2E)	$12.95	_____
_____	1-57248-112-9	How to Start a Business in PA (2E)	$16.95	_____
_____	1-57071-179-8	Landlords' Rights and Duties in PA	$19.95	_____
		TEXAS TITLES		
_____	1-57071-330-8	How to File for Divorce in TX (2E)	$19.95	_____
_____	1-57248-009-2	How to Form a Simple Corporation in TX	$19.95	_____
_____	1-57071-417-7	How to Make a TX Will (2E)	$12.95	_____
_____	1-57071-418-5	How to Probate an Estate in TX (2E)	$19.95	_____
_____	1-57071-365-0	How to Start a Business in TX (2E)	$16.95	_____
_____	1-57248-111-0	How to Win in Small Claims Court in TX (2E)	$14.95	_____
_____	1-57248-110-2	Landlords' Rights and Duties in TX (2E)	$19.95	_____

SUBTOTAL THIS PAGE _____

SUBTOTAL PREVIOUS PAGE _____

Illinois residents add 6.75% sales tax _____

Florida residents add 6% state sales tax plus applicable discretionary surtax _____

Shipping— $4.00 for 1st book, $1.00 each additional _____

TOTAL _____